BEADWORK®
Creates

D1009177

Beaded Bags

Edited by
Jean
Campbell

INTERWEAVE PRESS

Project editor: Jean Campbell
Technical editor: Marion Agnew
Illustrations and photo styling: Ann Swanson
Photography: Joe Coca
Book design: Paulette Livers
Book production: Samantha L. Thaler,
  Paulette Livers
Copy editor: Stephen Beal
Proofreader: Nancy Arndt

Printed and bound in China by Asia Pacific

Library of Congress Cataloging-in-Publication Data
Beadwork creates beaded bags: 30 designs / Jean Campbell, editor.
  p. cm.
  ISBN 1-931499-34-9
  1. Beadwork. 2. Handbags. I. Campbell, Jean, 1964-
TT860.B334 2003
646.4'8--dc21

                    2003004092

10 9 8 7 6 5 4 3 2 1

INTERWEAVE PRESS

201 East Fourth Street
Loveland, Colorado 80537-5655 USA
www.interweave.com

Dear Reader,

Do you consider your handbag a simple necessity? Well, take a seat at the bead table! You've got some rethinking to do. There's nothing like beads to spice up a wardrobe, and a beaded bag is a great first step. The thirty bags featured in this book will put you on the right track. A far cry from the rectangular amulet bags that were popular ten years ago, each one of these bags presents a totally new view of the words beaded + bag. The variety of shapes and colors will complement anyone's wardrobe, and the array of techniques—off-loom, loomwork, bead crochet, and bead knitting—is enough to keep every beadworker satisfied.

Before you start making your own beaded bag, be sure to check the Tips section on page 125. Another resource is the Techniques section on page 126, where each stitch used in the book is clearly defined. Together the illustrations and words will help you learn a new stitch or jog your bead-stitching memory.

So page through the beautiful projects and select your perfect bag. You're about to make a stunning fashion statement!

—Jean Campbell
Editor, *Beadwork*
magazine and books

Con

tents

Fancy Dress Bag

Jean Campbell

3¼" L x 1½" W (without fringe)

You're sure to get compliments when you wear this unusually shaped amulet bag festooned with fire-polished beads and pearls.

Materials

176 transparent topaz, olivine, and spring green 6 x 5 faceted fire-polished rondelles

14 transparent topaz faceted fire-polished teardrop beads

1 hank of 5mm golden freshwater pearls

5 olivine 2 x 25 Czech 2-holed tubes

Size 11° transparent topaz Japanese seed beads

Size 11° opaque olivine Japanese seed beads

Size B gold beading thread

Notions

Size 12 beading needle

Scissors

Step 1: Make the front of the bag. Using 2 yards of thread and leaving a 4" tail, create a strip of square stitch 10 rondelles wide by 15 rondelles long. The rondelles should lie vertically for each row. Work the colors randomly. Weave in the tail and working threads and trim.

Step 2: Make the back of the bag. Use the topaz size 11°s to create a strip of peyote stitch that is slightly larger than the square-stitched strip created in Step 1. The bag shown has a peyote-stitched strip that is 26 beads wide by 40 beads long.

Step 3: Assemble the bag. Begin by starting a new thread and whipstitch the two strips together at the sides. On the bottom, weave the thread from each bead on the peyote-stitched row to the connecting threads on the square-stitched row.

Step 4: Begin to embellish the top by starting a new thread at the top of the square-stitched row. Use pearls and olivine size 11°s to create simple fringe across the bag. Exit through the last

rondelle of the bag. *String 1 olivine tube, 1 topaz rondelle, and 1 olivine size 11°. Pass back through the rondelle and the tube. * Pass through all of the rondelles on the first row of the bag and repeat from * to *.

Weave through beads so you exit from the fourth end rondelle down. Repeat from * to *, using the second hole of the tube. Pass through the rondelles of the fourth row and repeat from * to *. Secure the thread and trim.

Step 5: Begin the bottom fringe by starting a new thread at the lower corner of the bag, exiting from the corner rondelle. String 1 olivine size 11°, 1 pearl, 1 olivine size 11°, 1 rondelle, 1 olivine size 11°, 1 teardrop, and 1 olivine size 11°. Pass back through all but the last bead strung. Pass through the rondelle you just exited and come out between the first and second rondelles. Make another fringe leg.

Pass through the second rondelle. String 1 tube and make a fringe leg. Pass back through all except the last bead strung. Pass through the third through eighth rondelles on the row. Pass through the second hole of the tube. Repeat the fringe sequence so it matches the first three fringe legs. Secure the thread and trim.

Step 6: Make the strap. Begin by starting a new 8" thread at the upper corner of the bag. *String 1 olivine size 11° and 1 pearl. Repeat from * twice.

String 6 olivine size 11°s and pass through a tube. String 5 olivine size 11°s and pass back through the first size 11° strung in this step. Weave through the whole stringing sequence several times. Secure the thread and trim.

Step 7: Repeat Step 6 on the opposite upper corner of the bag.

Step 8: Using a yard of thread, string 6 olivine size 11°s. Pass through the second hole of one of the green tubes added in Step 6. String 5 olivine size 11°s and pass back through the first bead strung in this step. Tie a knot.

String beads as desired using all of the pearls, fire-polished, and seed beads. String enough beads so the strap will reach your desired length, compensating for the tube on the oppo-

site side's length. When you are ready to attach the other tube, string 6 olivine size 11°s, pass through the second hole of the tube, string 5 olivine size 11°s, and back through the first seed bead added before the tube. Tie a knot. Pass through all of the beads on the strap again, tying knots periodically to secure the thread.

*Jean Campbell is the editor of **Beadwork** magazine and books.*

Travel Bag

Margo C. Field

1⅜" L x 2" W (without fringe)

You can make this little bag when you travel. Only one color of seed bead is required for the body of the bag, so there's no need to keep track of a pattern. When you reach your destination, make a strap and add the creative embellishments. A work of art!

Materials

Size 11° seed beads
Size 15° seed beads
Assorted accent beads
Size B beading thread in color to complement beads
Hook clasp

Notions

Size 10 and 12 beading needles
Paper towel roll (optional)
Beeswax or Thread Heaven

Step 1: Using about 2 yards of waxed single thread and leaving a 6" tail, string 48 size 11°s and tie in a circle. If desired, slip the circle of beads onto the paper towel roll or work with the circle of beads on your fingers.

Step 2: Work even count tubular peyote stitch for 1½". Remove the paper towel roll.

TOP

Step 3: *String 3 size 11°s, pass over the next space, and through the next. Repeat from * around to make 12 nets of three beads each. Pass up through the first two beads added in this step (Figure 1).

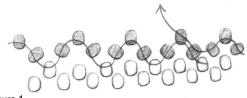

Figure 1

Step 4: *String 2 size 11°s. Pass through the second bead of the next net. Repeat from * around to make 12 nets of two beads each. Pass through the first two beads added in this step (Figure 2).

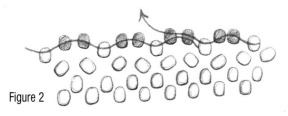

Figure 2

Step 5: *String 1 size 11°. Pass through the next two beads of the previous step. Repeat from * to add a total of 12 beads. Pass through the first bead added in this step (Figure 3).

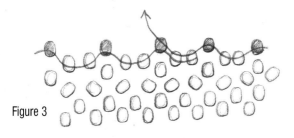

Figure 3

Step 6: Repeat Steps 4 and 5.

Step 7: Repeat Step 4. Weave the thread through several beads to secure, tie a knot if desired, pass through a few more beads, and trim.

BOTTOM

Step 8: Weave in the original tail thread and trim. Begin a new thread and exit from the first row of peyote stitch. Work one row of tubular peyote stitch.

Step 9: Repeat Step 3.

Step 10: *String 3 size 11°s. Pass through the second bead of the next net. Repeat from * around to make 12 nets of three beads each. Pass through the first two beads added in this step.

Steps 11 and 12: Repeat Step 10.

Step 13: Repeat Step 4.

Step 14: Repeat Step 5.

Step 15: Work around in tubular peyote stitch, adding 12 beads total. Pass through the first bead added in this step.

Step 16: *String 1 size 11° and pass through the next bead from Step 15. Skip the next space by directly passing through the next bead from Step 15 (don't pass into the beads of Step 14). Repeat from * around to add 6 beads total. Pull tightly. Pass through the first bead added in this step.

Step 17: Work around in tubular peyote for a total of 6 beads. Pull tight. Pass through the first bead added in this step.

Step 18: Repeat Step 17. The round should form a tight circle. Reinforce the circle a few times and weave the thread up to the base of the bag. Weave through several beads to secure, tie a knot if desired, pass through a few more beads, and trim.

Step 19: Start a new thread on the face of the bag. Create your own embellishment, making a dangle of simple and looped fringe using size 11° and decorative beads.

TASSELS

Step 20: Add fringed tassels as desired using the size 15°s and accent beads. The bags pictured have five long tassels and eight shorter tassels.

STRAP

Step 21: Anchor a 3-yard length of thread to one side at the top of the bag. String some large decorative beads and a section of size 15°s mixed in with some size 11°s to add texture. Repeat this sequence until you reach half of the desired strap length. End with a large bead sequence.

String a clasp and pass back through the large bead sequence. *String a seed bead section and pass through the next large bead sequence. Repeat from * until you reach the bag. A third strand of seed beads may be added. Add fringes and embellishments as desired along the strap. Adding extra embellishment helps reinforce the strap with the extra thread passes.

Step 22: Repeat Step 20 on the other side of the bag. At the point where you added the clasp on the previous strap, you will add a series of looped sections using size 15° and size 11° beads (Figure 4). The loops should be big enough for your clasp to fit through—they make the length of your bag strap adjustable. The sample shows nine loops; the more loops you add, the more the length of the strap can vary. Reinforce the loops at least three times by repeating the thread path.

Figure 4

Step 23: Finish the end with several larger or decorative beads.

Margo C. Field "discovered" beads in 1990. After retiring from a career in hospital pharmacy, she opened Poppy Field Bead Company in Albuquerque, New Mexico. She teaches classes at her store and workshops across the United States.

Handle Connection

Nancy Geddes

4" L x 5" W

Do you have a soft crocheted or knitted bag that you're itching to give a handle? Here's a unique solution on how to work a beaded handle from something soft.

Materials

- Assortment of beads
- 2 beads with large holes to fit over crimp beads
- Crimp beads
- Purse's yarn
- Soft Flex beading wire
- Glue
- Size B beading thread in color to match bag
- 2 jump rings
- Lanyard clip or lobster claw clasp

Notions

- Crochet hook appropriate for yarn
- Size 12 beading needle
- Crimping pliers

Step 1: Crochet a single chain rope with the purse's yarn. You will double this rope to make part of the handle. When you're planning the length of the handle, take into consideration that in addition to the doubled rope there will be 12" of beading.

After crocheting the rope, double it and attach the ends to one another by weaving the tail into the chain and dabbing a little glue on the bottom of the woven ends.

Step 2: Sew a jump ring 1" down from the top on each side on the inside of your purse.

Step 3: Take the chain rope and fold it in half with the woven end near the center (top).

Step 4: Using a 10" piece of beading wire, string a crimp bead and pass through one of the chain rope's ends. Pass back through the crimp bead and squeeze.

Step 5: String the beads for 6", using the large-holed bead first. The first bead needs to go over the crimp and hug securely to the crocheted handle, but it shouldn't be so large that it passes up the crocheted section.

Step 6: String a crimp bead and a lanyard clip or lobster claw. Pass back through the crimp bead and several of the beads on the wire. Pull tight and squeeze the crimp bead (Figure 1).

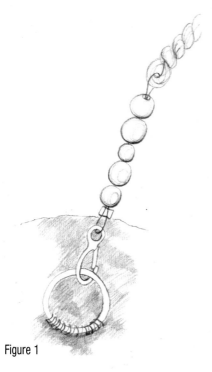

Figure 1

Step 7: Repeat Steps 5–7 for the other end of the crocheted rope chain.

Step 8: Clip the handle to the rings in the purse.

Nancy Geddes loves to knit and crochet but is mainly a bead maker and glass fuser specializing in dichroic glass. Her jewelry is known for luminescence and strong design.

Terrifically Tacky Tote

Jean Campbell

4⅜" H x 6⅞" W x 3⅛" D

You'll love making this little tote! Not only does it bring instant gratification, but it will bring compliments as well.

Materials

> Hanks of size 11° seed beads in an
> assortment of colors
> Assortment of 3mm–7mm accent beads
> Clear plastic box with a handle
> 1" wide Terrifically Tacky Tape

Notions

> Large scissors
> Small sharp scissors
> X-acto knife

Step 1: Completely cover the plastic on the box with the tape. Keep the protective layer of the tape on. Use the knife to cut the tape to the exact measure as you maneuver around the edging, the handle, and the latch.

Step 2: Remove a section of the protective layer on the tape. Press accent beads into the tape as desired.

Carefully pull out one of the strands from a hank. Lay the strand—beads and thread—on the tape. Keep the strand in orderly lines or circles, do a free-form design, or work around your accent bead design. Always

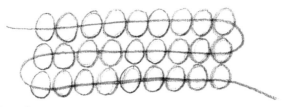

Figure 1

butt one line of the strand up to another (Figure 1). While keeping the thread in the strand, firmly press the seed bead design into the tape. If possible, carefully pull out the thread from the strand of beads. If the thread won't pull, use the small scissors to trim the thread very close to the work.

Step 3: Repeat Step 2, completely covering the box with beads. The tape should cure completely between 24 and 72 hours, or until the beads are firmly stuck.

Jean Campbell is the editor of **Beadwork** *magazine and books.*

Moss Garden Purse

Barbara L. Grainger

2½" L x 5" W

Here's a sweet little treat to carry a credit card and keys or to use as a business-card holder. The finished purse is 3" × 5". If you desire a larger purse, simply enlarge the pattern.

Materials

> Size 11° transparent dark green and transparent light green seed beads
> Size 11° and 14° silver-lined kelly green, olive, magenta, and transparent bronze seed beads
> Size 6° seed beads in color(s) of your choice
> 8" x 8" pieces of dark green velvet and dark green silk
> Size B green beading thread
> Paper

Notions

> Scissors
> Pins
> Fabric marker
> Size 12 beading needles

Step 1: Use a piece of paper to copy the pattern on Figure 1, enlarging the pattern until it reaches the actual purse size. Cut on the drawn lines and discard section B. Pin section A to the right side of the velvet. Trace both the inside and outside lines onto the velvet with a pen or marker.

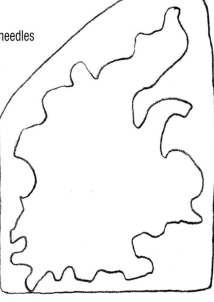

Figure 1. Enlarge this pattern 225%.

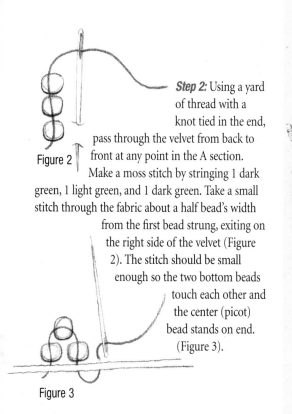

Figure 2

Step 2: Using a yard of thread with a knot tied in the end, pass through the velvet from back to front at any point in the A section. Make a moss stitch by stringing 1 dark green, 1 light green, and 1 dark green. Take a small stitch through the fabric about a half bead's width from the first bead strung, exiting on the right side of the velvet (Figure 2). The stitch should be small enough so the two bottom beads touch each other and the center (picot) bead stands on end. (Figure 3).

Figure 3

Step 3: Repeat Step 2. Work randomly, exiting the fabric at different angles to change the direction of the beads so the work takes on the look of moss. Crowding the beads is encouraged since you don't want the fabric to show through the beads. Make blends in some areas by using 1 dark green, 1 olive, and 1 dark green for a few stitches. Then string 1 dark green and 2 olive for a few stitches. Finally, use 3 olive and work stitches until you are ready to change colors again. The result is a smooth color blend. Work the new color until you feel the need to change, then introduce one of the other colors into the mix. For added texture and interest add a size 6° as the middle bead. To achieve a high and low effect, switch to size 14°s for a while, working in the same color scheme. Continue adding new colors and repeating old colors until area A is completely beaded.

Step 4: Carefully cut the excess velvet, leaving a ½" seam allowance. With wrong sides together, lay the purse on the silk lining fabric and trace the purse's shape with a pen or marker. Cut out the lining. Place the two fabrics together, wrong sides touching, turn in the seam allowances, and pin into place.

Make the lining about ¹⁄₁₆" smaller than the velvet so the lining stays inside the purse. Sew together with small whipstitches.
Step 5: Fold the bottom of the purse up and sew the sides closed. If necessary, work more moss stitches on the sides to cover the seam. Work a few strands of moss over the edge of the flap onto the underside if desired.

Barbara L. Grainger is an internationally recognized beadwork author, instructor, and designer who specializes in innovative beadwork techniques.

New York Cage

Jean Campbell

4¾" L x 8½" W x 1½" D

This project was inspired by a Garment District window display I saw in New York. It's an easy way to turn a plain purse into something that'll knock your socks off.

Materials

- 14- and 18-gauge silver wire
- Bali beads and spacers
- Liquid silver beads
- Assortment of hematite beads
- Black sewing thread
- Rectangular plain black purse

Notions

- Wire cutters
- Flat-nose pliers
- Round-nose pliers
- Sewing needle
- Scissors

Step 1: Lay the 14-gauge wire across the bottom of your purse, leaving a 2" tail. Make a 90-degree bend at the corner opposite from the wire's end. Continue around the perimeter of the purse, making bends at the corners. When you reach the last corner, cut the wire 2" past the bag. Make spiral loops on each of the end wires and twist them together, maintaining a 90-degree angle (Figure 1).

Figure 1

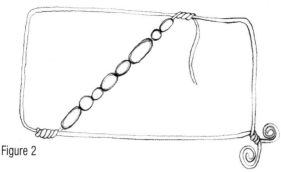

Figure 2

Step 2: Cut an 8" length of 18-gauge wire and begin a coil at one edge of the wire rectangle (Figure 2). String beads separated by liquid silver—enough to reach the other edge of the wire rectangle. Coil this beaded wire around the 14-gauge wire and continue adding beads, weaving back and forth on the rectangle. Also weave from one 18-gauge length to another.

If you find you need more wire for weaving, simply end the old wire by coiling it off and trimming it close to the coil. Start a new wire by repeating this step.

Continue until you feel you have a nice web of wire and beads.

Step 3: Cut three 4" lengths of 14-gauge wire. Bend each in half. Make a small spiral at each end.

Step 4: Twist the pieces you made in Step 3 around the corners that don't have these embellishments.

Step 5: Sew the cage to the front of the purse body.

Jean Campbell is the editor of **Beadwork** *magazine and books.*

Art Deco Evening Bag

Robyn Lakeman

5¼" L x 5" W (without fringe)

Here's a beautiful bag to bring you back to the elegance and sophistication of the 1920s. The beaded portion is made using loomwork, and the satin body is stitched on.

Materials

Size 11° seed beads in Crystal Pharoah Blue, Emerald Green, Aquamarine, Crystal Buttercup, Lemon, Black Opaque, Crystal Candy Pink, Crystal Black, Rainbow Orchid, Crystal White, and Crystal Pale Blue

Size B beading thread

Leukoplast (sticky bandaging material)

1 yard of black satin

Purse frame

Notions

Bead loom

Size 10/13 beading needle

Scissors

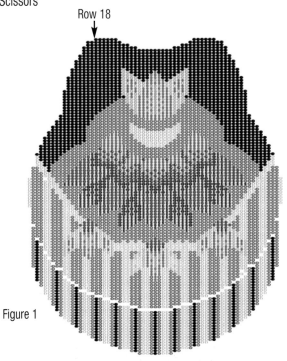

Row 18

Figure 1

LOOMWORK

Step 1: Follow the chart (Figure 1) to weave the bag's body. Start from Row 18 and work back to Row 1. Begin again by knotting the thread at the bottom of Row 18 or the right side of the loom. Pass through the row and exit from the top of Row 18 or the left side of the loom. Continue working the pattern for the remainder of the bag. When you have completed weaving, take your piece off the loom, cut the warp threads to 3" and apply Leukoplast to the top of the threads. Fold them underneath and press onto the back of the beadwork. Trim the Leukoplast at the outer points and cut off excess warp threads.

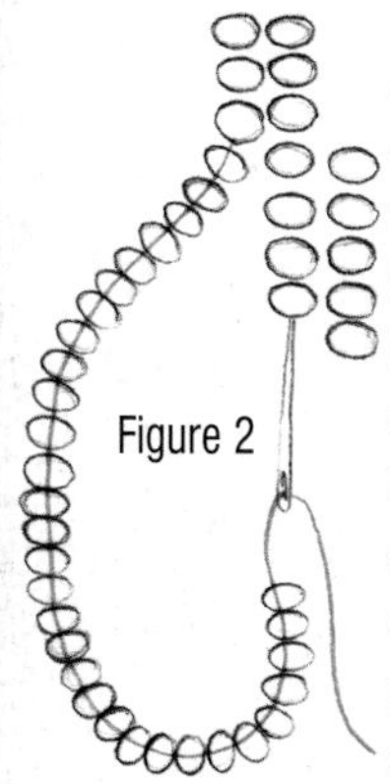

LOOPED FRINGE

Step 2: Start a new thread, knotting it between the last and second-to-last bead at the bottom left side of the beadwork. Pass down through the bottom bead and string the first fringe loop according to Figure 2 (the figure shows half the loop). Pass back up through the last bead of the second row of the bag and down through the third row of the bag. String the next loop of fringe, pass up into the fourth row of the bag and down through the fifth. Repeat as before. Continue across, following the pattern, until the fringe is complete. Secure the thread in the body of the bag and trim close to work.

Figure 2

ASSEMBLY

Step 3: Using the beaded piece as a pattern, cut three pieces from the satin; add a ¼" seam allowance to all of the edges. Use two of the pieces and make the right sides face. Stitch a ¼"-wide seam, leaving a space to turn the completed piece inside out. Place the right side of the third pattern piece of satin together with the front of the beaded piece. Sew the two together with the bottom open. Turn inside out and sew the bottom closed. Tuck in the allowance. Place the two remaining pieces of satin together, right sides facing, and sew around; leave a small opening on the seam. Turn inside out and sew closed. With satin pieces facing, stitch the double piece of satin onto the back of the beaded piece up to where the purse frame will be placed. Sew the top sides of the bag individually onto the purse frame.

Robyn Lakeman of Aqua Unicorn Images began beading in 1993. Robyn wrote a book **Beaded Chokers & Bracelets** *with her partner Ton Gerritsma in 1994, and produced beading patterns that are sold throughout Australia.*

Barbara

Sheilah Cleary

10" L x 5" W (without tassel)

This wonderful 1920s-era bag was inspired by an antique piece found in Southern California. Don't be afraid of the bead crochet—the bag uses beads of one color, so you can simply and quickly transfer strands of beads to your thread.

Materials

   6 hanks of size 11° seed beads
   7 cards of YLI silk buttonhole twist to match beads
   Batting
   Ribbon or cord to match beads

Notions

   Size 8 crochet hook
   Size 13 crochet hook
   Tapestry needle
   Scissors
   Fray Check

Note: Read all instructions before beginning.

PREPARING THE BEADS AND THREAD

Don't untie your bead hanks. They are tied so you can gently pull on a strand close to the knot to release it from the hank.

Unwind 5 yards of thread. Tie one strand of beads to the silk thread (Figure 1). Carefully slide the beads onto the thread. Push the beads all the way along the 5 yards of thread. Wind the beaded thread onto the card and leave several feet of unbeaded thread. Put a second strand of beads on the thread in the same manner. Add a third strand plus half a fourth strand. This should be enough beads per card for the body of the bag. This could be misleading as one card and 3½ strands would not be enough to complete the body of the bag. If you

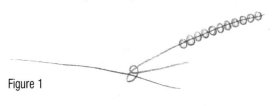

Figure 1

run out of beads you may unwind the unbeaded thread and strand on the number of beads you need.

Begin a new thread for the fringe area of the pattern. Do this just before ending the row before the fringe row. Be sure you have enough beaded thread to complete the fringing row. Don't knot off during the fringing row. Load a full hank of beads onto this card of thread before beginning.

Throughout this project, any time you join two strands of beaded thread it is imperative that you use Fray Check to seal the knot. Apply a small amount on the threads that you weave in as well.

ABBREVIATIONS
(ch) chain
(bch) bead chain
(bsc) beaded single crochet
(bdc) beaded double crochet
(btr) bead triple crochet
(dc) double crochet
(inc) increase
(dec) decrease
(sc) single crochet
(ss) slip stitch
(tr) triple crochet

BODY
Round 1: Ch12, join to make a circle.
Round 2: Ch3 (counts as 1tr), 2 more tr in same space. 3tr in each chain st around (36 st), join with ss.
Round 3: 3bch (counts as 1btr), 2btr in next st, 1btr in next st, 1bch, *skip 1 st, 1btr, 2btr, 1btr, 1bch. Repeat from * around and join. You should have 9 sections of 4btr with a bch separating each section.
Round 4: 3bch (counts as 1btr), 1btr, 2btr, 1btr, 1bch. *Skip the bch from the round below, 1btr, 2btr, 1btr, 1btr, 1bch. Repeat from * around and join. You should have 9 sections of 5btr separated by a bch. These sections must stack exactly on top of the sections from the round below and each bch should line up on top of another.

Continue around increasing 1btr in each section for each round. Make the increase in or near the center of the section.
Round 5: 3bch (counts as 1btr), 1btr, 2btr, 1btr, 1bch. *6btr in each section separated by a bch. Repeat from *

around and join. Remember to do the 3bc after joining and count that as 1btr.

Round 6: 7btr in each section separated by a bch. Make sure the sections line up.

Round 7: 8btr in each section separated by a bch.

Round 8: 9btr in each section separated by a bch.

Round 9: 10btr in each section separated by a bch.

Round 10: 11btr in each section separated by a bch.

Round 11: 12btr in each section separated by a bch.

Round 12: 13btr in each section separated by a bch.

Rounds 13 and 14: Repeat Round 12. Work even 13btr in each section separated by 1bch.

Round 15: Insert the hook into the next st as though to sc. Slip 4¼" of beads along the thread up to your work. Yarn over just beyond the beads and pull through stitch, yarn over and complete your sc. Be sure that all the slack is pulled up from the loop of beads. It's very important that you don't pull the loop up too tightly. It needs to be very flexible. Repeat this process with each stitch around including the bch stitches.

Round 16: Repeat Round 12. Make sure the sections line up.

In the next rounds, make the decrease near the center of each section. To decrease, leave out one of the triples.

Round 17: 12btr in each section separated by a bch.

Round 18: 11btr in each section separated by a bch

Round 19: 10btr in each section separated by 1bch.

Rounds 20–24: Work 10btr in each section separated by 1 bch.

Rounds 25 and 26: 4bch, *skip 1 st, 1btr in next st, 1bch. Repeat from * around. Join at third bch.

Round 27: *1bsc, 1bdc, 1bdc, 1btr in each of the next 5 stitches, 1bdc, 1bdc, 1bsc. Repeat from * around and join. Make sure that each bch lines up with the bch stitches from Round 24.

Round 28: *1sc, 1sc, 1bsc, 1bdc, 1bdc, 2bdc in next st (inc), 2bdc in next st (inc), 1bdc, 1bdc, 1bsc, 1sc. Repeat from * around and join. Note that the sc (unbeaded) stitches are made over the 2bsc from the row below.

Round 29: ch1, 1sc in each st around. Join and finish off thread.

BALL

Make two.

Round 1: Using the size 13 hook, ch4 and join.

Round 2: 8bsc in center of circle, do not join.

Round 3: 2bsc in each st around (16 st).

Round 4: 2bsc in next st, 1bsc in next st around (24 st).

Rounds 5–9: 1bsc in each st around.

Round 10: *1bsc in first st, skip next st, bsc in next 2 st. Repeat from * around (16 st).

Round 11: *1bsc in first st, skip next st, bsc in next st. Repeat from * around.

Fasten off, leaving a 10" tail (you have to use it later). Thread the tapestry needle with fastened-off thread and make a running st around the circle. Stuff lightly with small amount of batting. Do not pull the thread tight; leave the needle attached.

FINISHING

To finish the purse, choose grosgrain ribbon, double-sided satin ribbon, or any cord of your choice. Cut the ribbon into two sections and weave through the ribbon round (Rounds 25 and 26). Weave one round with the ends exiting from one side of the purse and the second round exiting from the other. Keep the ribbons neat and untwisted. Weave through two btr for ribbon and one btr for cord. Tuck both ends of the ribbon from one side into one of the beaded balls. Use the tapestry needle to draw up the circle on the beaded ball and sew around, sewing into the ribbon several times. Repeat with the other ribbon using the other beaded ball.

BOTTOM FRINGE

Attach a new thread in original chain at the bottom of the bag. With right side facing you, insert the hook through 1 chain. Measure 5" of beads, yarn over just beyond the beads and pull up loop, yarn over and draw thread through both loops on hook. Continue around, placing 1 beaded loop in each chain around. Finish off and sew in thread securely. Use Fray Check on the finished thread.

An international tutor and bead artist, Sheilah Cleary has been a crafter all her life. She can be reached at shebeads@aol.com or go to www.shebeads.com.

Don't Bug Me!

Pat Mayer

12½" L x 17¼" W

What a breeze! Find a printed fabric you love and use the design to create a beautiful embellishment with beads.

Materials

Size 11° seed beads in colors that match the colors of
   your fabric
Accent beads to match print theme
1 yard of tapestry-weight fabric with bold design
1 yard of heavy cotton fabric in color to complement
   print
48" of ½" cord piping
32" of 1" webbing
Size B beading thread to complement beads
Sewing thread to complement the fabric
Masking tape

Notions

Size 12 beading needle
Sewing needle
Scissors
Sewing pins
Sewing machine

Step 1: Cut out the pattern pieces (Figure 1) and tape the edges with masking tape to prevent fraying.

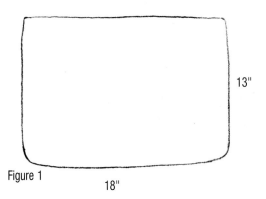

Figure 1

13"

18"

Step 2: Work beaded backstitch over the existing design of the fabric on each pattern piece. Stay inside the edges enough for the ½" seam allowance.

Step 3: Assemble the bag. Use a zipper foot to avoid sewing over the beads. Lay the unbeaded bag piece right side up. Lay the cord piping around the bag's edge, with the piping to the inside and the band of the piping lined up with the edge of the fabric. Lay the beaded bag piece, beaded side down, on top. Pin. Sew through all three layers around the sides and bottom of the bag, next to the piping. Turn right side out.

To assemble the lining, pin right sides together along the sides and bottom. Sew sides and bottom. Insert the lining into the bag.

To hem the top edges of the bag and lining, turn them down and blind stitch by hand, leaving room at the edges to insert the ends of the strap, which is made in the next step.

Step 4: Work a long peyote-stitched strip 1" wide by 32". If you're forming letters, use odd-count peyote stitch so they will center.

Hand sew the beaded strip to the webbing, wrong sides together.

Sew the strap to the corners of the bag (Figure 2). Attach embellishing beads to the inside of the strap.

Figure 2

Pat Mayer lives in Hollywood, Florida. Among the many joys that have come to her through beading are the love of the creative process, the beauty of the beads, the fun of the hunt, and the wonderful friendships made with kindred spirits she has met along the beading path.

Southern Plains Strike-a-Light Pouch

David Dean

5⅛" L x 3¾" W (without fringe)

This type of bag was designed by Native Americans to carry fire-making tools. Along with beads, thread, needles, and other European goods, the tin cones that line the edge were once objects of trade. The Strike-a-Light pouch was usually one in a set of bags that carried all the tools a Native woman needed for her day-to-day chores. The bags were decorated differently from tribe to tribe. The Kiowa often beaded a small design on the back of the bag even though it was not seen. The purpose was to give the creator/user of the bag something that was hers alone. The Cheyenne usually beaded these bags in a lane-stitch design in geometric patterns. The Kiowa and Comanche used two-needle appliqué that depicted abstract floral patterns. Many older bags were made from the tops of U.S. military boots. Men also carried Strike-a-Light pouches, but they didn't employ tin cones and featured just straight or twisted fringe.

Materials

- Size 13° red, blue, orange, and yellow charlottes
- 12 silver 6mm round beads
- 2 white 1½" hair pipe beads
- 34 tin 1" cones
- 36 tin ¾" cones
- 4 tin 3" cones
- Silver concho with button-type shank
- 4 small cowrie shell jingles
- 4" x 8" piece of black cowhide
- 35 thin strips of natural buckskin 1" long, 4 strips 20" long, and 1 strip 18" long
- Size B Nymo beading thread
- Jeweler's glue

Notions

    Size 12 sharps needle
    Scissors
    Pliers
    Hole punch or awl

Step 1: Follow the charts on Figure 1 to trace and cut out the pieces of the bag from the cowhide.

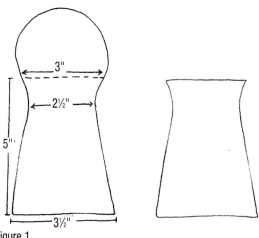

Figure 1

Step 2: Using lane stitch, follow the pattern on Figure 2 on the body and flap of the bag, leaving a ½" seam allowance.

Step 3: Place the two pieces with the wrong sides together. Line up the bottom edges. Use small whipstitches to sew the pieces together, leaving the curved flap and the bag's opening free. Bead over the seam as necessary to keep the pattern.

Step 4: Work a row of fringe along the bottom using the tin cones. Begin by cutting a 2" strip of buckskin. Punch 19 holes along the bottom edge of the bag (through both pieces of the leather). The center 17 holes will have a uniform tin cone fringe; the two outside holes will have cowrie and longer tin cones. For the 17 center holes, tie a knot at the end of a 2" strip of buckskin. Thread a 1" tin cone on it and pinch the cone with the pliers so the knot catches the cone. Pass the strip through one of the holes and repeat for the other end so that a cone dangles from either side of the bottom of the bag.

Using two 20" lengths of buckskin twisted together, thread and

fasten a 3" cone; the "pinch" will come about 6" from the end. Thread the other end through the punched hole on one end of the bottom of the bag, leaving about 1½" of twisted buckskin between the top of the tin cone and the bag. Tie a knot, snugging it up to the bottom of the bag. Leave about 1" of buckskin from the knot, thread and pinch another 3" cone. About 1½" from the bottom of the buckskin, tie an overhand knot. Separate the two twisted threads and tie a cowrie shell onto each end. Repeat at the other corner so you have four long fringes.

Step 5: Work the fringe along the flap. Punch 36 evenly spaced holes along the flap of the bag. Cut eighteen 3" to 3½" lengths of buckskin. Thread one piece down through the first hole and up through the second; attach the ¾" tin cones the way you did for the bottom fringe. Continue along the edge. Each fringe should emerge from the top of the buckskin.

Figure 2

Figure 3

Step 6: Punch a hole in the center of the front flap large enough to accommodate the shank. Cut a strip of buckskin the length you want your strap to be plus another 6". Push the shank of the concho through the center hole while threading the buckskin through the first hole punched in the back of the bag, through the shank of the concho, and back out through the other hole, leaving the ends at the top (Figure 3). The strap holds the concho in place. On each end, string 3 silver beads, 1 hair pipe, and 2 silver beads. Tie the top of the handle together.

David Dean is an avid beadworker and author of Interweave Press's **Beading in the Native American Tradition***. He lives in Englewood, Ohio, with his family.*

Sioux Pipe Bag

David Dean

23¼" L x 6½" W (without fringe)

Pipe bags are used among Native Americans to store the accouterments for the ceremonial and leisurely consumption of tobacco. Historically, each tribe developed its own style and pattern for a pipe bag. Shown is a Sioux pipe bag featuring lane-stitch beadwork and a section of quillwork.

Materials

Size 11° seed beads in white, navy, yellow, kelly green, and red

16" × 20" piece of brain tanned or commercial tanned elk or buckskin

16½" × 8" piece of buckskin

8" × 8" piece of thin rawhide

Size B white beading thread

Prepared porcupine quills in red, navy, and yellow

Water

Glue

Notions

Size 12 sharps needle

Pen

Scissors

Razor knife

Bowl

Tablespoon

BAG

Step 1: Fold the 16" × 20" piece of buckskin in half lengthwise. Hand-sew the long sides together with a straight seam. Turn the bag inside out so the seams don't show. Also, turn a 1" hem at the top and whipstitch.

Step 2: Transfer Section 1 of the chart (Figure 1) to the front of the bag. The lanes drawn should be ½" each. Do the same for the back of the back using Figure 2. Use lane stitch to bead the front, back, sides, and upper edges of the bag.

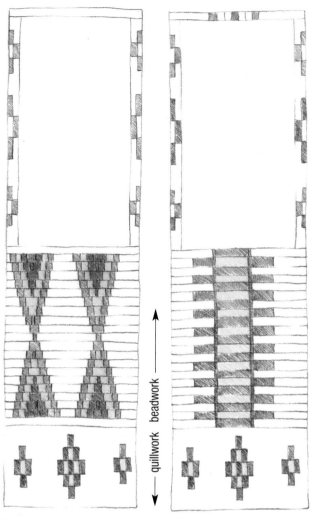

Figure 1   Figure 2

← quillwork   beadwork →

QUILLWORK

Step 3: The second section is quillworked. Use the razor knife to cut the thin rawhide in ¼" strips, leaving a ¼" at the top and bottom of the rawhide so the strips stay connected. Soak the quills in a bowl of water until they are pliable. Flatten each quill by placing it under the backside of a tablespoon. Press down hard on the spoon and pull the quill through.

Follow Section 2 of the chart (Figure 1) for color placement. Hold the end of the quill so it is slightly angled to the rawhide slat (Figure 3). Tightly wrap it around the slat so the end is tucked under the wrap (Figure 4) at the back side of the work. Continue wrapping so no rawhide shows. When you reach the end of the quill, begin a new one, folding the tip of the new

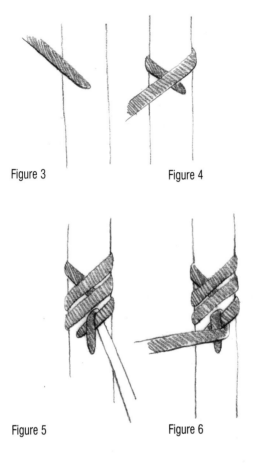

Figure 3   Figure 4

Figure 5   Figure 6

quill over the end of the previous one (Figure 5). Wrap it around to secure (Figure 6). Though the quills at the back of the slat are angled, they should lie straight across the front. The completed slat can be flattened further with a tablespoon.

FRINGE

Step 4: Cut strips on the remaining piece of buckskin each ¼" wide. Leave a ½" border at the top.

ASSEMBLY

Step 5: Insert the quillworked section about ¼" into the bottom of the bag. Flat stitch the quillworked section to the front and back bottom of the bag so the bag closes. Place a line of glue along the top of the fringed piece of buckskin. Wrap it around the bottom of the quillworked section.

David Dean is an avid beadworker and author of Interweave Press's **Beading in the Native American Tradition**. *He lives in Englewood, Ohio, with his family.*

Black Filigree Bag

Lindsay DeGree

8⅜" L x 4¾" W

There'll be plenty of oohs and ahhs when you wear this fantastic bag.

Materials

- 5–7 hanks black size 15° seed beads
- 250–300 black size 3mm and 4mm glass faceted beads
- Size D thread or size .014 Soft Flex beading wire
- ¼ yard of lightweight black rayon fabric
- Black size B beading thread
- Black sewing thread

Notions

- Scissors
- Sewing needle or sewing machine
- Embroidery hoop
- Size 12 beading needle

Step 1: Cut the fabric into four 5" × 9" rectangles. Two will be the bag and two will be the lining. For the bag, lay out two rectangles with right sides together. Sew one of the short sides and both of the long sides together. Use ¼" seams and leave ¼" to turn under at the top. Repeat the sewing steps for the lining.

Step 2: Bead embroider the filigree design (Figure 1) on one side of the bag.

Step 3: Along the bottom seam of the bag, attach 20 legs of simple fringe. Alternate legs of A and B fringe:

Figure 1. Enlarge this pattern 30%.

Pattern A: 14 seed beads, 3mm glass bead, 5 seed beads, 4mm glass bead, 5 seed beads, 3mm glass bead, 10 seed beads, 4mm glass bead, seed bead.

Pattern B: 14 seed beads, 3mm glass bead, 5 seed beads, 4mm glass bead, 5 seed beads, 3 mm glass bead, 16 seed beads, 4mm glass bead, seed bead.

STRAP
Step 4: String enough 4mms to equal 44". *String 11 seed beads and a 3mm, skip one 4mm bead on the initial strand, and pass down through the next two 4mms. Repeat from * for the length of the initial strand.

ASSEMBLY
Step 5: Insert the lining in the bag, wrong sides together. Turn ½" of the raw edges to the inside and sew a seam ¼" from the top. Sew the spiral strap ends to each corner of the bag inside the top seam allowance. Blind stitch the top edge closed. Embellish the top edge with seed beads and glass 3mm beads.

Lindsay DeGree began beading seven years ago and continues to broaden her horizons in the world of beads and bead embroidery. Currently attending college, she is employed at the Bead Cache in Fort Collins, Colorado.

Evening Out

Shelley Hauge Wong

3⅝" L x 3¼" W (without fringe)

This evening bag is made with the contemporary minimalist in mind. There's just enough room for lipstick, credit card, and enough cab fare to get home. Store the bag in an embellished silk organza pouch to protect it when it's not out and about.

The design was influenced by a textile pattern. It has rhythm, balance, repetition, and a wonderful play of color, in addition to a rich texture of beads created by mixing matte, shiny, AB, and lined beads. The ensemble received an honorable mention at the Great Northern Beadwork 2002 Exhibit juried by Jo Wood.

Materials

Delicas in light topaz (101), topaz (065), peridot (903), amethyst (782), violet bronze (1054), raspberry iris (104), and purple (004)

4mm and 5mm amethyst bicone Austrian crystals

3mm lime bicone Austrian crystals

10mm Venetian glass bead

8mm octagonal faceted amethyst crystal

Size 8° violet bronze seed beads

Size 2 violet bronze bugle beads

Silamide in color to complement beads

Purple iridescent organza drawstring bag

Notions

Size 12 beading needle

Scissors

Tube of lipstick

BODY

Rows 1–3: Using a yard of thread and leaving a 4" tail, string 124 beads following the color chart (Figure 1); begin at the

Figure 1

top. Work in a tube or start with three rows of flat peyote and then join the ends to form a circle.

Rounds 4 and on: Follow the chart working in tubular peyote stitch.

Fold the tube in half and stitch through the "up" beads like a zipper. Reinforce the bottom by weaving through the beads across the bottom.

Make a loop for the clasp by weaving through the beads and exit from a bead just below the second center square of the pattern. Exit two beads from the edge of the square, string 21 seed beads of violet bronze, and enter two beads from the edge of that square.

FLAP
Rows 1–17: Begin a new thread at the top corner of the bag. Work flat peyote stitch across the back of the bag, following the chart (Figure 2).

Rows 18–28: Work a flat peyote square in the center of the flap.

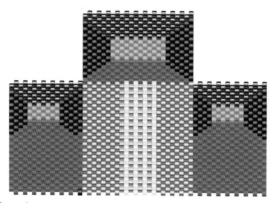

Figure 2

CLASP

Exit between the sixth and seventh "up" beads at the end of the flap. String 1 violet bronze seed bead, 1 lime crystal, 1 purple octagonal faceted bead, the Venetian glass bead, a lime crystal, a 5mm amethyst bicone, a lime crystal, and a violet bronze seed bead. Pass back through all but the last seed bead strung and secure the thread in the flap.

FRINGE

Begin a new thread at the bottom corner of the bag. *String 10 violet bronze seed beads, a 4mm bicone purple, 3 violet bronze seed beads, a lime bicone, 3 violet bronze seed beads, a 5mm bicone purple, 3 violet bronze seed beads, a lime crystal, and 1 violet bronze seed bead. Pass back through all except the last seed bead strung. Pass through the next bead on the bottom of the bag. Repeat from * across the width of the bag.

STRAP

Following the color chart (Figure 3), make a strap 6 beads wide and 48" long using flat peyote stitch. Sew the strap ends to each top corner of the bag by weaving through beads on the body of the bag.

LIPSTICK COVER

Using a yard of thread and leaving a 4" tail, make an alternating pattern of 2 violet bronze and 2 purple seed beads. String enough to wrap around the line marking the opening of the lipstick tube. Tie a square knot to make a circle and pass through the first bead. Work down the long end of the tube in tubular peyote stitch.

Figure 3

When you reach the top edge, decrease to cover the top and add a crystal in the center of the top. Embellish the edges of the top with a simple fringe of lime crystals and seed beads.

ORGANZA BAG

For embellishment, work bugles and size 8°s in spot stitch in loose rows all over the fabric. Using seed stitch, add a row of seed beads around the drawstring hem.

Shelley Hauge Wong lives in Minneapolis, Minnesota. She has loved playing with beads for many years and became a serious beader in January 2000 when she took her first formal class. The obsession has had her in its grip ever since.

Off to Market

Jamie Hogsett

9½" L x 15" W (without handle)

Knit this beautiful market bag using delicious cotton and ribbon yarns and candy-like resin beads. The result is something stunning that you can carry a substantial stash in!

Materials

- 3 skeins Mission Falls 1824 Cotton in Fennel 301
- 3 skeins Berroco Zen in Mushi Gray 8215
- 8 strands of 8mm resin beads in green, light gray-blue, light olive, dark olive, aqua, and lavender in various shapes
- 2 strands 18mm–30mm light gray-blue and light green round and teardrop-shaped resin beads

Notions

- Size 8 and 17 knitting needles
- Sewing needle with a large hole
- Tapestry needle
- Scissors

BOTTOM

Using both yarns held together, cast 3 stitches onto size 8 needles.

Rows 1–23: Knit 1, yarn over, knit to the end of the row. Repeat until you have 25 stitches on the needles.

Rows 24–74: Knit every row.

Row 75–97: *Knit 1, knit 2 together, knit to end of row. Repeat from * until you have 3 stitches on the needles.

Bind off (Figure 1).

SIDES

Note: These are worked from the bottom up.
Using the sewing needle, string half of the
small resin beads onto one skein of the ribbon
yarn. Using both yarns held together and size 17
needles, cast on 38 stitches.

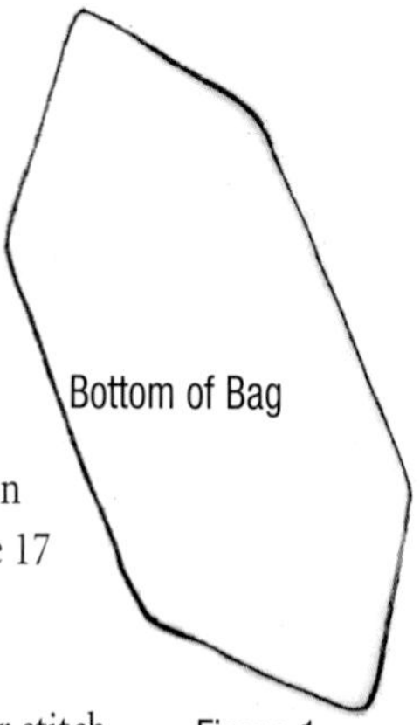

Row 1: Knit row without adding any beads.
Row 2: Knit row, adding a bead to every other stitch.
Rows 3–10: Repeat Rows 1 and 2 five times.
Rows 11–17: Knit 7 rows without adding any beads.
Row 18: Knit, adding a bead every 5 stitches.
Row 19: Knit.
Row 20: Knit, adding a bead every 3 stitches.
Row 21: Knit.
Rows 22–33: Repeat Rows 18–21 three times.
Rows 34–39: Knit.
Row 40: Knit, adding a bead to every other stitch.
Bind off.

Bottom of Bag

Figure 1

Repeat above to create the other side of the bag.

SEAMS

Thread three strands of the ribbon yarn, held together, onto
the tapestry needle. Pass around and through the first holes,
attaching the sides of the bag to the bottom. Pass through a
few times and move on to the next holes in the sides and
bottom.

Using one strand of the ribbon yarn and one strand of the
cotton, seam the sides together using whipstitch.

Weave in all yarn ends.

HANDLES

Use the tapestry needle to first string the large beads onto two
strands of the ribbon yarn. Then thread the sewing needle
with one strand of ribbon yarn and pass through the beads
already strung. Repeat with the last strand of ribbon yarn. Tie
a large knot between each bead, making sure the knot is right
next to the beads. Tie the handle to the top of the bag in the
same place as the corners on the bottom of the bag. Weave the
ends straight down into the bag to add needed strength to the
area that is pulled by the handle.

Jamie Hogsett is editorial assistant of **Beadwork***.*

Windows of Spring

Jeri Herrera

2½" L x 2" W (without fringe)

This springlike amulet bag displays a riot of color and lush foliage. The holes in the face of the bag are a special challenge for peyote-stitch lovers.

Materials

Delicas in light teal, dark teal, metallic gold, grass green, forest green, and assorted flower colors

Size B Nymo beading thread in color to complement beads

Notions

Size 10 long needle

Scissors

Paper towel roll

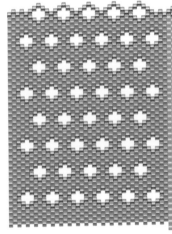

Figure 1

Step 1: String 38 dark teal and 36 light teal. Tie in a circle. Cut a paper towel roll and size it to fit the circle. Follow the chart (Figure 1). The white areas on the chart are holes. To make the holes, weave through existing beads

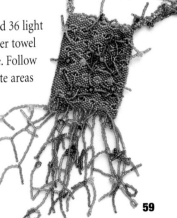

to reach the place where you need to add a bead (Figure 2). Fold the tube in half and lock the beads together. Stitch together like a zipper.

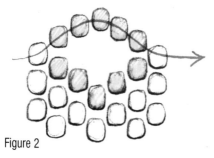

Figure 2

Step 2: Make a strap of your choice using the teal and gold. Attach each end to the top corners of the bag.

Step 3: Start new thread in back of the bag and come out of the bottom corner hole. Use shades of green to make vinelike strands that have offshoots. Do so by stringing a length of beads and then making simple fringe off the strand (Figure 3).

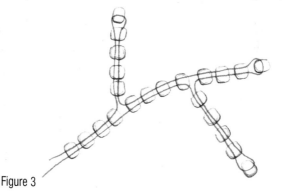

Figure 3

Continue the vine, weaving it in and out of the holes of the bag. Add flowers along the way and at the end of the vines. Flowers are made by stringing 1 yellow, *1 red, and passing through the yellow. Repeat from * until you've added 6 red. Add a drop of Fray Check to secure. Change the color of the flowers as you go.

Step 4: Work a row of fringe along the bottom of the bag using branch fringe and adding flowers as desired.

Jeri Herrera has been beading for the last nine years. She also enjoys teaching in her local community. You can reach Jeri via e-mail at jherrera@wwdb.org.

Trinity Handbag

Paulette Livers

6¼" L x 5" W

The beautiful triad patterning on this bag reminds us that good things often come in threes.

Materials

- 140 yards (40 grams/1.4 ounces) 100% mercerized cotton; Crystal Palace Yarns Baby Georgia Wedgwood blue
- Sturdy thread to match the cotton
- 270 size 6° square or pony beads
- Accent beads slightly larger than the size 6° beads
- Old silk necktie

Notions

- Scissors
- 9" long #1 wooden knitting needles
- Sewing needle

Abbreviations: k = knit; sl1= slip 1 bead with next knitted stitch

BAG

Rows 1–31: String 270 size 6° on your mercerized cotton. Cast on 31 stitches. Knit all rows.

Row 32: k3, sl1, k1, sl1, k1, sl1, k5, sl1, k1, sl1, k1, sl1, k5, sl1, k1, sl1, k1, sl1, k3.

Row 33: Knit across.

Row 34: Repeat Row 32.

Row 35: Knit across.

Row 36: Repeat Row 32.

Rows 37–43: Knit across.

Rows 44–80: Repeat Rows 32 through 43 nine times or until your piece measures about 12".

FLAP

Row 1: *k1, sl1, k2, sl1. Repeat from * to the end of the row, end k1.

Row 2: Knit across.

Row 3: *k2, sl1, k1, sl1. Repeat from *, end k1.

Row 4: Knit across.

Repeat these four rows until the flap measures about 2½", or about 40 rows total.
Rows 41 and 42: Knit across. Cast off.

LINING

Open the necktie so it lies flat and iron it. Trim the fabric to fit the body of the bag and sew it onto the knitted piece with wrong sides together. Fold the piece (Figure 1) and sew the sides of the bag together, avoiding the flap.

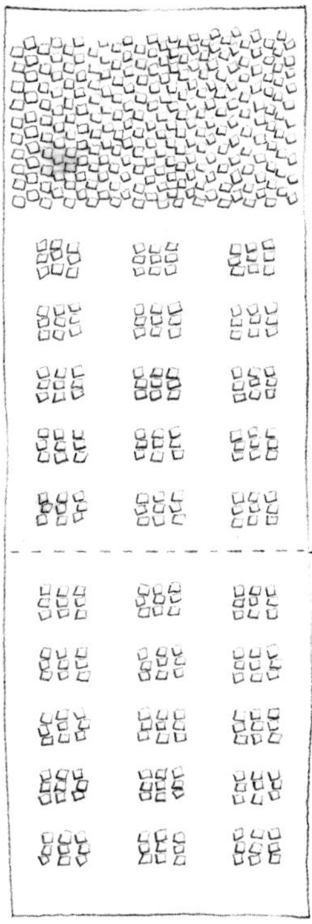

STRAP

Cut four 64" lengths of yarn. Tie the strands together at one end. Thread 18 accent beads onto two of the strands, evenly spaced. *Twist two strands, one with accent beads, one without, to the end. Repeat to make two twisted cords. Twist these two twisted cords together to the end. Repeat from * to make four cords. Make some with more or fewer beads scattered within. Join all the cords together to make one big twisted cord. Do so by twisting two cords, then the other two, and finally the sets of two together. Sew the large twisted cord to the side of the bag on each side of the flap opening. Allow the cord ends with accent beads to dangle outside the bag and slide the cord ends without accent beads to the inside of the bag.

← fold

Figure 1

Variation on the Trinity Handbag

Paulette Livers, a freelance graphic designer and illustrator in Boulder, is also the designer of Beadwork magazine. Her love of arts and crafts spans painting, beading, knitting, and just about any creative venture that falls in her path.

Tooth Fairy Bag

Dustin Wedekind

2¼" L x 1¾" W

What sort of purse would the tooth fairy carry? A beaded one, of course! Put a tooth in this bag, leave it under the pillow, and it's sure to attract a winged nighttime visitor.

Materials

Size 11° white seed beads
Size 11° gold seed beads
Size D beading thread
22-gauge wire

Notions

Size 11 beading needle
Scissors
Wire cutters

Step 1: String 3" of white beads and tie in a knot. Pass through the first bead and work tubular peyote stitch for 1". Begin decreasing one stitch each row along the sides and work another ¾".

Step 2: At the front of the bag, string 7 beads and pass through a bead at the back of the bag. Work peyote stitch around, using this bridge as a foundation row for a smaller tube of peyote—the root of the tooth. Work a decrease in every round to taper the tube to a point. When the tube is down to three beads around, end the thread and trim close to work. Start another thread near the bridge and work a second tube that is thinner than the first.

Step 3: Start a new thread at the top of the bag. Work a flat piece of peyote stitch along the back edge of the bag to form the flap. After three rows begin decreasing on each edge, finishing each decreased row with a gold bead. Work down to a point. End the thread and trim close to work.

Step 4: Cut a 6" piece of wire and fold it in half. Pass both ends through the side of the bag near the top, from the inside out, with a bead or two between them. String gold beads over both wires together. Pass the other end of the folded wire through the other side of the bag from the outside to the inside and twist the ends to secure them inside the bag.

Dustin Wedekind is the managing editor of **Beadwork** *magazine.*

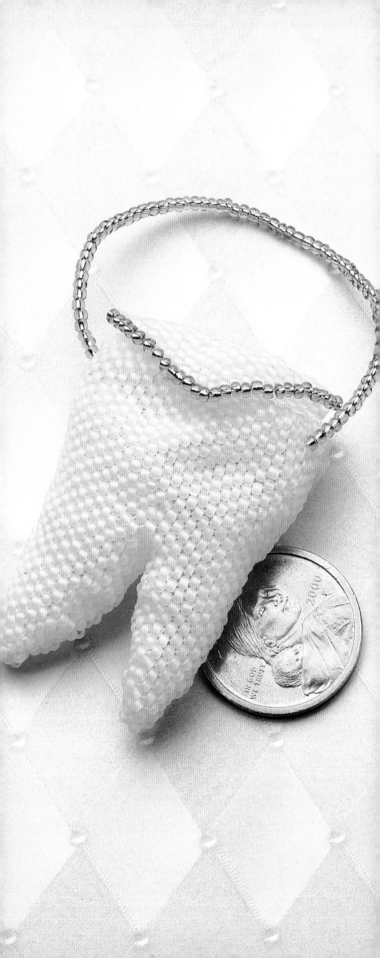

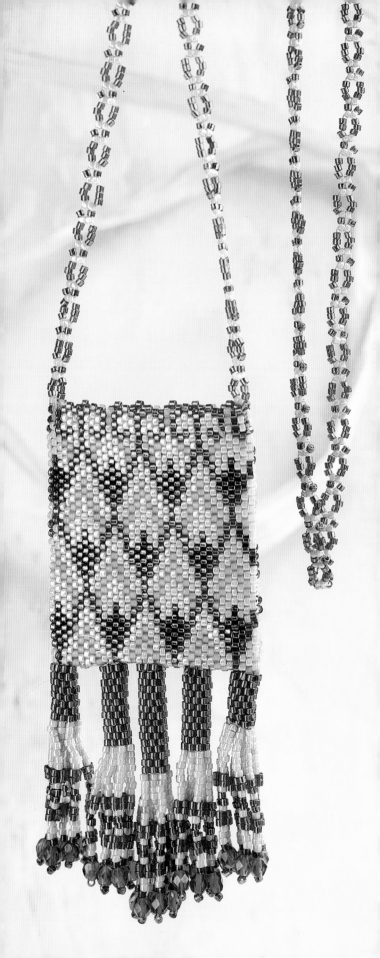

Tapestry Amulet Bag

Janie Warnick

2" L x 1¾" W (without fringe)

This is no run-of-the-mill amulet bag! With its unique tassels and stunning pattern, it's sure to make people stop and stare.

Materials

- Delica beads in Ceylon beige, matte transparent pale yellow, silver-lined olive, and silver-lined teal
- 35 teal 4mm faceted glass beads
- Size B beading thread in color to complement beads

Notions

- Size 12 beading or sharps needle
- Scissors

BODY

Step 1: Using a yard of thread and leaving a 6" tail, work the chart from bottom to top (Figure 1) in tubular peyote stitch. Work the final round by weaving through the beads from the previous rounds until you reach the crest of the scallop. Place the olive bead to form the peak of the scallop and weave through the beads to the next crest.

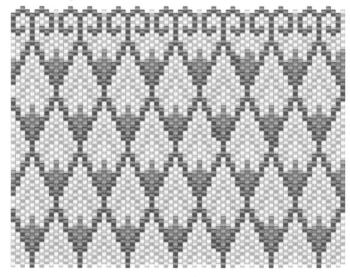

Figure 1

Start a new thread at the bottom round. Collapse the beaded tube in half. Stitch the bottom beads together like a zipper. Tie a knot between the beads. Weave the working and tail threads through several beads to secure and trim. Set aside.

TASSELS

Step 2: Using a yard of thread and leaving a 4" tail, work flat peyote with olive beads. Make the strip 8 beads wide by 14 beads high.

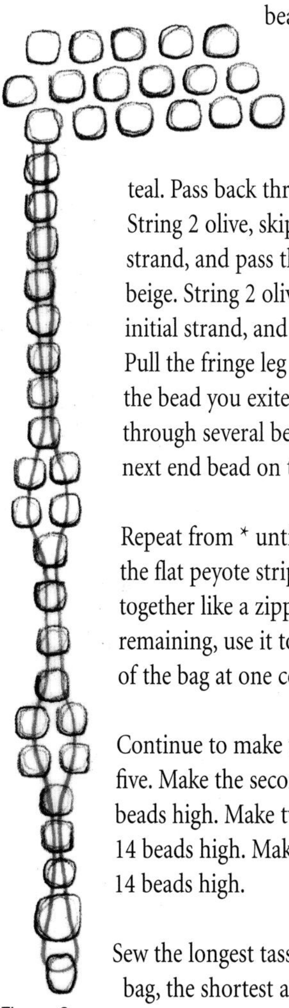

*String 8 beige, 2 olive, 1 beige, 2 teal, 1 beige, 2 olive, 2 beige, 1 teal, one 4mm, 1 teal. Pass back through the 4mm, 1 teal, 2 beige. String 2 olive, skip the next 2 olive on the initial strand, and pass through 1 beige, 2 teal, and 1 beige. String 2 olive, skip the next 2 olive on the initial strand, and pass through the final 8 beige. Pull the fringe leg snug (Figure 2). Pass through the bead you exited on the strip. Weave up through several beads and down through the next end bead on the strip.

Repeat from * until you have 7 fringe legs. Fold the flat peyote strip in half and sew the edges together like a zipper. If there is enough thread remaining, use it to sew the tassel to the bottom of the bag at one corner.

Continue to make tassels until you have a total of five. Make the second tassel 8 beads wide by 14 beads high. Make two that are 12 beads wide by 14 beads high. Make one that is 16 beads wide by 14 beads high.

Sew the longest tassel to the bottom center of the bag, the shortest at the other bottom corner, and then sew the last two tassels between the center and end tassels as shown.

Figure 2

STRAP

Step 3: Work the strap with either one or two needles. Begin a new thread (or threads) at one of the top corners of the bag.

Two-Needle Method: String 2 beige on both needles. *String 1 teal on the left needle and 1 teal and 2 beige on the right needle. Pass the left needle through the 2 beige. String 3 olive on the left needle. String 3 olive and 2 beige on the right needle and pass the left needle through the 2 beige. Repeat from * to reach the desired length, ending with two beige beads (Figure 3). Secure the thread at the other top corner of the bag.

Figure 3

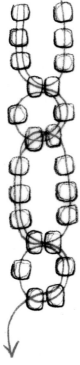

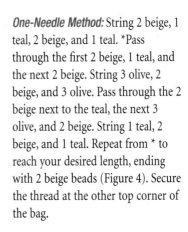

One-Needle Method: String 2 beige, 1 teal, 2 beige, and 1 teal. *Pass through the first 2 beige, 1 teal, and the next 2 beige. String 3 olive, 2 beige, and 3 olive. Pass through the 2 beige next to the teal, the next 3 olive, and 2 beige. String 1 teal, 2 beige, and 1 teal. Repeat from * to reach your desired length, ending with 2 beige beads (Figure 4). Secure the thread at the other top corner of the bag.

Yesterday, Janie Warnick sewed, embroidered, and quilted. Today, she beads.

Figure 4

Emese's Bag

Robin Atkins

4½" L x 4½" W

This little bag is designed to hold a small treasure, coins, jewelry, or special amulet. The feminine shape is attractive with or without loopy fringe embellishments. You may follow the beading plan as shown in the sample, or make changes in the colors and/or design to suit your own taste.

Materials

3 pieces of quilting-weight plain or print cotton fabric, 5" × 8" each
Lightweight acid-free paper, 5" × 8"
Sizes 5°–15° seed beads in your preferred color palette
Size 1 bugle beads
Tiny drop beads
1" Chinese coin or stone donut
5 glass 10mm heart beads
Sewing thread in contrasting color
Nymo D beading thread in a neutral color
Facial tissue

Notions

Scissors
Sharp pencil
Sewing needle
Size 12 beading needle
Notebook/typing paper

Step 1: Using acid-free paper and the pattern at Figure 1, trace the bag. Be sure there is ½" of blank paper all around the shape.

Step 2: Choose one of the three pieces of fabric for the surface of the bag. (The other two will be used for the lining and the pocket.) Place the back side of the paper against the wrong side of the fabric and pin them together at the corners. Following your traced outline of the bag shape and using small running stitches with contrasting thread, baste through both the paper and fabric. Also baste the fold line.

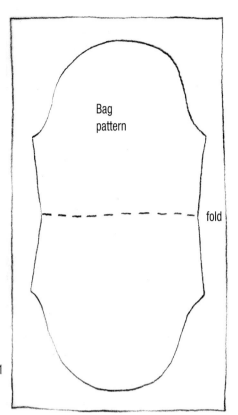

Bag
pattern

fold

Figure 1

Step 3: Begin to bead on the fabric, staying within the basted outline. Stitch through both the paper (which will keep your work from puckering) and the fabric. Using back stitch, sew a line of beads all the way around the outside edge of the bag (just inside the basted outline). Place the coin (or donut) in the center of the bag front and couch it down with the neutral thread. Using couching, lazy, seed, and back stitches, and following the design on the sample (or creating your own), cover the entire front and back of the bag with beads.

Step 4: When you have completed the bead embroidery, prepare the bag for lining. Use a moist tissue to dampen the paper along the original basted outline. Carefully tear away the outer edge of paper so only the cloth remains in the seam allowance area. (The paper will remain under your beading stitches.) Cut around the outside of the bag, leaving a ½" seam allowance. Slightly clip the seam allowance at the fold line and along the inward curves on each side, being careful not to clip into the basting stitches. Fold in the seam allowance and finger press. If the seam doesn't stay in place, baste the seam allowance with large temporary stitches. It may be helpful to baste along the outside of the curved edges and snug the stitches slightly to pull the seam allowance evenly inward (Figure 2).

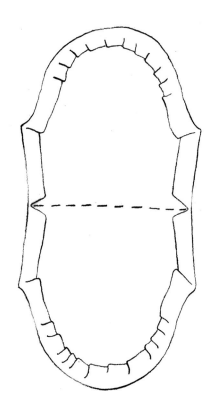

Figure 2

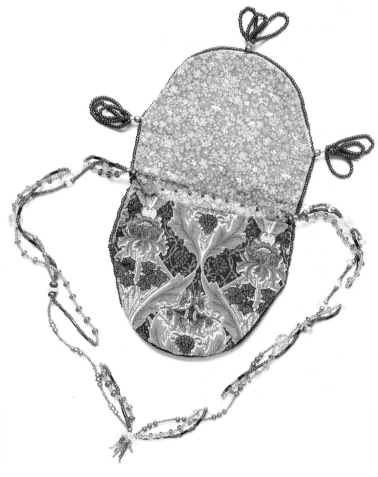

Step 5: Using typing or notebook paper, trace the bag pattern exactly the way you did at the start. Draw a ½" border around the bag outline for the seam allowance. Choose one of the remaining pieces of fabric for the lining. Pin the traced pattern to the fabric and cut out the lining around the outer edge. Clip at the fold line and finger press the fold. Use small whipstitches to attach the lining to the bag, with the seam allowances of both pieces facing each other. Adjust the seam allowance folds on the lining as needed to exactly match the bag.

Step 6: Make the pocket using the same pattern as for the lining. Cut the pocket from the remaining piece of fabric with a ½" seam allowance all around. Fold the pocket fabric in half at the fold line, right sides together. Using small running stitches (or a sewing machine) and a ½" seam allowance, sew from the fold line halfway around. Leave a 1½" space at the bottom center and continue sewing to the fold line. Turn the pocket

inside out through the opening. Gently poke the corners at the fold to make sure they're turned completely. Using small whipstitches, attach the pocket to the lining. Be sure to place the pocket on the underside of the bag, so that when the front is folded down it covers the pocket.

Step 7: To finish the bag, use the seed stitch to place a small "dotted" line of beads along the fold on the inside. Sew through both the lining and the beaded piece. Take care that the stitches don't show on the beaded side. Sew three loopy fringes at the center of the bag front and repeat at each of the corners.

STRAP

If you desire to make a strap, sew flower-shaped beads inside the fold of the purse at the corners. Make a strap of your choice and attach the ends using embroidery thread looped around the flower-shaped beads.

HINTS

- Don't run lines of beads along or closely parallel to the fold line. If you do, the fabric will show when the bag is folded. It's better to design the pattern so that the lines of beads run diagonally across the fold line.
- To prevent your sewing thread from tangling, don't make the loopy fringe in the hole of the coin (or donut) until you've completed all the other beading.
- To achieve some texture on the front of the bag, you can make little stacks or short loops of beads. Use less texture on the back side of the bag.
- If you wish to make the bag slightly larger or smaller than the sample, use a copy machine to enlarge or reduce the pattern.

Robin Atkins, bead artist, teacher, writer, and lecturer, has been delighting in beads since childhood and creating with them as a career since 1988. She made Emese's Bag as a tribute to her Hungarian godchild, Emese Varga.

Sophisticated Squares

Lori Kindle

8¼" L x 7½" W (without tassel)

Elegant but simple, the pattern for this bag consists of one
large square knitted piece and four smaller ones. Put together
with straps and a tassel, the piece has a 1920s look and feel.

Materials

- 5 hanks of size 10° black iridescent square seed beads
- 32 size 10 square cut black crystal bicones
- Size 8 black pearl cotton
- Two 10" x 10" pieces of black silk
- Size B black Nymo beading thread
- Batting

Notions

- Size 0000 knitting needles
- Beading needle
- Sewing needle
- Size 10 crochet hook

LARGE SQUARE
Make one.
String all the beads on the yarn. Using the beaded yarn, cast
on 71 stitches.

Row 1: Slip 1 stitch, slide 1 bead in place as you knit each
remaining stitch as follows: insert right needle into the next
stitch in preparation to knit it, slide a bead close to the needle,
then knit the stitch as usual. The bead will be on the back side
of the work, between the last two stitches worked.

Row 2: Slip 1 stitch, knit to end.

Rows 3–84: Repeat Rows 1 and 2. Your work should now
measure approximately 8" × 8".

Bind off.

SMALL SQUARE
Make four.
Using the beaded yarn, cast on 35 stitches.

Row 1: Slip 1 stitch, slide 1 bead next to each remaining stitch as before.

Row 2: Slip 1 stitch. Knit to end.

Rows 3–46: Repeat Rows 1 and 2. Your work should now measure approximately 4" × 4".

Bind off.

HANDLE STRAPS

Using the beaded yarn, cast on 6 stitches.

Row 1: Slip 1 stitch, slide 1 bead next to each remaining stitch.

Row 2: Slip 1 stitch, slide 1 bead next to each remaining stitch.

Note: Beads will appear on both sides of your work.

Repeat Rows 1 and 2 until your work measures 16" long.

Bind off.

Repeat the process above to create a second strap.

SLIDE RING STRAP

Using the beaded yarn, cast on 3 stitches.

Row 1: Slip 1 stitch, slide 1 bead next to each remaining stitch.

Row 2: Slip 1 stitch, slide 1 bead next to each remaining stitch.

Note: You will once again be working beads onto both sides.

Repeat Rows 1 and 2 until the work is 8" long.

Bind off.

SLIDE RING

See the instructions for bead crochet rope on page 133 in "Techniques." Using the crochet hook and the beaded yarn, make a 4" crocheted rope. Join the two ends together by using a beading needle to connect and weave in the ends for a neat circle.

TASSEL

Using the beaded yarn, cast on 8 stitches.

Row 1: Slip 1 stitch, *slide 2 beads next to each remaining stitch, knit 1. Repeat from * across, end last repeat knit 2.

Row 2: Slip 1 stitch, knit into the back and front of each of the next 6 stitches (to make increases), knit 1 (14 stitches total).

Row 3: Slip 1 stitch, *slide 2 beads next to next stitch, knit 1. Repeat from * across, end last repeat knit 2.

Row 4: Slip 1 stitch, knit across.

Row 5: Slip 1 stitch, *slide 2 beads next to next stitch, knit 1. Repeat from * across, end last repeat knit 2.

Row 6: Slip 1 stitch, *knit into the back and front of the next stitch, knit 1. Repeat from * across (26 stitches total).

Row 7: Slip 1 stitch, *slide 2 beads next to next stitch, knit 1. Repeat from * across, end last repeat knit 2.

Row 8: Slip 1 stitch, knit across.

Rows 9 – 20: Repeat Rows 7 and 8 six times.

Row 21: Slip 1 stitch, *knit 2 together, repeat from * to the last 2 stitches, knit (12 stitches total).

TASSEL FRINGE

Row 1: Slip 1 stitch, *knit into the back of the next stitch, sliding 100 beads in place as you do so, then knit into the front of the same stitch, also sliding 100 beads in place, repeat from * to the last stitch, knit 1. This will leave you with 20 loops and 22 stitches.

Row 2: Slip 1, *knit 2 together repeat from * to the last stitch, knit 1 (12 stitches).

Row 3: Repeat Row 2 for 7 stitches remaining. Bind off.

Use the yarn tail to pull the bottom tightly together. Sew up the side and gather the top. Use a bit of batting to fill out the top of the tassel. Secure with yarn.

LINING

Using the large square and one of the small squares as a pattern, cut out one piece of lining for each of the five squares. Leave a ½" allowance for the seams.

ASSEMBLY

Begin with two small squares. Place the wrong sides together and use yarn to whipstitch the two smaller squares together, only stitching half way up the side. Repeat with the other two squares. Open these two pieces and with wrong sides together and the two seams lined up, sew the two pieces together on one long side. Again, only sew half

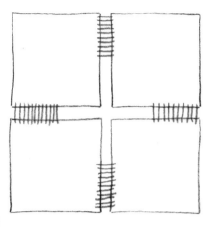

Figure 1

the length of the squares from the outside edge toward the center. When you open the piece (after the four half seams) it will look like one big square but the inside corners will fold back to create the opening for the bag (Figure 1).

Take the large square and the four connected squares and put their right sides together. Sew the two large squares together all around the outside.

Connect the slide strap to the slide ring. Making sure that the strap doesn't twist, sew the handle strap ends to each of the four corners of the top opening of the bag, catching the slide strap in the seam in one of the four corners. Sew the tassel to the center of the bottom of the bag.

TRIM

Use the beading needle and thread to anchor your thread at one corner of the bag. *String 14 size 10°s, 1 crystal, and 14 size 10°s. Pass into the bag at the edge about an inch from where you last exited to create one loop. Repeat from * around the bag to create a row of looping fringe. When you have reached the starting point, find the center of the first loop and secure your thread there. You now make a series of shorter loops. String 20 beads and secure at the midpoint between loops. Continue around bag.

Sew the lining fabric together as you did the body of the bag but with the right sides together; use an iron to press back the seam allowance. With wrong sides together, insert the lining into the bag. Sew around the opening of the bag, turning under the raw edge of the lining. The slide ring slips down over the handles to keep the bag closed.

Lori Kindle is from Sheridan, Wyoming, where she lives with her wonderful husband of thirty years. He is in full support of her bead habit.

Dance Bag

Nancy Zellers

3" L x 1½" D

This bag holds all the things your mama made sure you had when you left the house for a party. So loop the strap over your wrist and let's go dancing!

Materials

- 15 gr black matte Delicas
- 15 gr white shiny Delicas
- 5 gr bright 24kt gold-plated Delicas
- One 5mm gold-plated round bead
- One 2.5mm gold-plated round bead
- Size D black, gold, and white Nymo beading thread

Notions

- Size 10 beading needle
- Scissors
- Beeswax or Thread Heaven

Step 1: Using a yard of black thread and leaving a 4" tail, string 92 black. Tie a knot to make a circle. Work the chart (Figure 1) in tubular peyote stitch. Use black thread in the solid black areas and change to white thread in the other areas.

Step 2: Make two. Work the circular peyote-stitched bottom using a yard of doubled black thread and all black beads. Always pass through the first bead or beads added in each round to position your needle for the next round.

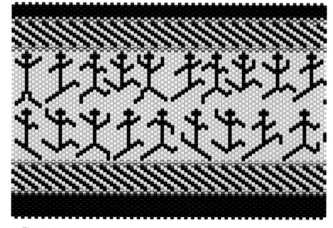

Figure 1

Round 1: String 3 beads and tie a knot to make a circle.

Round 2: Add 2 beads between each bead of Round 1 for a total of 6 beads.

Round 3: Add 1 bead between each bead added in Round 2 for a total of 6 beads.

Round 4: Add 2 beads between each bead added in Round 3 for a total of 12 beads.

Round 5: Add 1 bead between each bead added in Round 4 for a total of 12 beads.

Round 6: Add 1 bead between each bead added in Round 5 for a total of 12 beads.

Round 7: Add 1 bead between each bead added in Round 6 for a total of 12 beads.

Round 8: Add 2 beads between each bead added in Round 7 for a total of 24 beads.

Round 9: Add 1 bead between each pair of beads added in Round 8, passing through each pair as though they were one bead. This will total 12 beads added.

Round 10: Add 3 beads between each bead added in Round 9 for a total of 36 beads.

Round 11: Add 1 bead between every 3 beads added in Round 10, passing through each set of three beads as though they were one bead. This will total 12 beads.

Round 12: Add 3 beads between each bead added in Round 11 for a total of 36 beads.

Round 13: Add 1 bead between each three-bead set added in Round 12 for a total of 12 beads.

Round 14: Add 4 beads between each bead added in Round 13 for a total of 48 beads.

Round 15: Add 1 bead between each four-bead set added in Round 14 for a total of 12 beads.

Round 16: Add 5 beads between each bead added in Round 15 for a total of 60 beads.

Round 17: Add 1 bead between each five-bead set added in Round 16 for a total of 12 beads.

Round 18: Add 5 beads between each bead added in Round 17 for a total of 60 beads.

Round 19: Add 1 bead between each five-bead set added in Round 18 for a total of 12 beads.

Round 20: Add 6 beads between each bead added in Round 19 for a total of 72 beads.

Round 21: Add 1 bead between each six-bead set added in Round 20 for a total of 12 beads.

Step 3: Stitch one of the flat circular pieces made in Step 2 to the tube made in Step 1. Force the six-bead sets into the toothed peyote-stitched format so the two edges can be

locked together like a zipper. Adjust the spacing of the beads as necessary to compensate for the fact that the bottom has 84 beads on the outer edge and the bag has 92 beads. The natural decreases will pull the tube in slightly and round out the bottom edge. Weave through the beads several times to reinforce the connection.

Step 4: Make the edge of the bag lid using tubular peyote stitch.
Rounds 1 and 2: Using a yard of black thread, string 96 black. Tie a knot to make a circle. These two rounds are dummy rounds and will be removed later.
Rounds 3 and 4: Work around using gold.
Rounds 5–13: Work around using black.
Round 14: Work around using white.

Remove the first two rows of black dummy beads and reinforce the gold beads with the thread from the dummy rows.

Step 5: Stitch the second flat circular piece made in Step 2 to Round 14 of the tube made in Step 4. Do so by passing through 4 white from the tube and 1 black from the circle all the way around. Weave through all the beads again to reinforce.

Step 6: Make the ruffle. Always pass through the first bead or beads added in each round. Keep the thread well conditioned.
Round 1: Using white thread, string 3 black and tie into a circle.
Round 2: Add 2 white between each bead added in Round 1 for a total of 6 beads.
Round 3: Add 1 black between each bead added in Round 2 for a total of 6 beads.
Round 4: Add 2 white between each bead added in Round 3 for a total of 12 beads.
Round 5: Add 1 black between each bead added in Round 4 for a total of 12 beads.
Round 6: Add 2 white between each bead added in Round 5 for a total of 24 beads.
Round 7: Add 1 black between each bead added in Round 6 for a total of 24 beads.
Round 8: Add 1 white between each bead added in Round 7 for a total of 24 beads.
Round 9: Add 1 black between each bead added in Round 8 for a total of 24 beads.
Round 10: Add 1 white between each bead added in Round 9 for a total of 24 beads.
Round 11: Add 1 black between each bead added in Round 10 for a total of 24 beads.

Round 12: Add 1 white between each bead added in Round 11 for a total of 24 beads.

Round 13: Add 2 black between each bead added in Round 12 for a total of 48 beads.

Round 14: Add 1 white bead between each bead added in Round 13 for a total of 48 beads.

Round 15: Add 1 black between each bead added in Round 14 for a total of 48 beads.

Step 7: Stitch the ruffle made in Step 6 to the center of the lid. Do so by passing up through the lid and ruffle. String the 5mm, the 2.5mm, and a gold Delica. Skipping the Delica, pass back through all again. Weave through all again and reinforce on the lid.

Step 8: Make a spiral rope to use for the strap. Begin by using doubled gold thread and stringing 1 gold, 3 black, 1 gold, and 3 white. Pass through the first five beads strung to make a circle.

*String 3 black, 1 gold bead, and 3 white. Pass through the second gold on the previous circle to make another circle. Pass through the black and gold beads just strung.

String 3 white, 1 gold, and 3 black. Pass through the gold bead on the previous circle, and the white and gold beads just strung.

Repeat from * until the strap is 10½" long. Pass through all the beads on the spiral rope to reinforce them.

Step 9: Sew the rope to the bag's body. Match a gold bead at one end of the rope to a gold bead on the first round of gold on the body. Attach the other end of the rope in similar fashion on the other side of the bag.

Step 10: Fashion a keeper chain for the lid by making a strip of ladder stitch 1 bead wide by 2" long. Use black beads and black thread. Attach one end of the chain to the inside of the bag just under the lid rim. Attach the other end inside the rim.

Nancy Zellers is currently designing a series of black-and-white bags. You can reach her at spsnoz2276@aol.com.

Lotus Bag

Dustin Wedekind

9" L x 6" W

Create this bag's lotus pattern using three lines of beading to create a rich effect. You can do the same with any simple line drawing.

Materials

Two strands of freshwater pearls
Size 11° seed beads in blue, bronze, and clear
Size 15° seed beads in two blues and bronze
3mm blue pearlescent round beads
Two 10" x 6" pieces of purple/bronze silk fabric
Two 10" x 6" pieces of flannel fabric
10" x 12" pieces of bronze silk lining fabric
Size D beading thread
Sewing thread
Yarn or ribbon

Notions

Size 11 beading needles
Sewing needles or sewing machine
Scissors
Transfer paper

Step 1: Use the transfer paper to copy Figure 1 to a piece of purple/bronze silk. Use the sewing thread to baste a piece of flannel to the back.

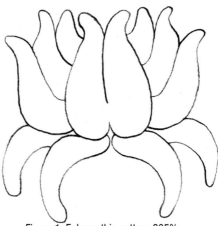

Figure 1. Enlarge this pattern 265%.

Step 2: Secure a yard of beading thread to the back of the fabric and use seed stitch to follow the line drawing with the pearls. Space them about ⅛" apart.

Step 3: Work a line of size 15° beads along the inside of the line of pearls using back stitch.

Work a second line of size 15°s in another color along the outside edge of the pearls.

Step 4: Baste an outline of the bag with sewing thread. Layer the front and back pieces, right sides together, with the flannel on the outside. Hand stitch, or use a sewing machine to follow the outline, sewing through the four layers of fabric. Don't sew the top.

Step 5: Turn the bag right-side out and trace it onto the lining fabric. Cut out and sew the lining pieces together; leave the top open. Place the lining inside the bag and blind-stitch along the top edge; fold the fabrics under.

Step 6: Make the loops and fringe. Begin a thread 1" below the top of the bag. String 7 seed beads, one blue pearl, one pearl, one blue pearl, and 7 seed beads. Pass through the fabric then * back through the beads to form a loop. Pass through the fabric and beads again to exit the bottom of the loop. String 2–3" of seed beads, 1 pearl, and one seed bead. Pass back through the pearl and string another 2–3" of seed beads plus the 1" of beads for the next loop. Pass through the fabric 1" from the top and repeat from * all around the bag.

Step 7: Make a picot edging across the top of the bag to hide the seam. Do so by using a yard of thread and clear size 11°s. Pass through the fabric from wrong to right side and string 3 beads, take a stitch in the fabric one bead's width, and *pass back through the last bead strung. String 2 beads and take a stitch. Repeat from * around the seam.

Step 8: Braid yarn and/or ribbon to make two pieces 12" long. Weave one through the loops and tie the ends in a knot. Repeat for the second piece, going in the opposite direction. Use beading thread to cover the knots with beads by exiting the top of the knot, stringing size 11° beads, and passing up through the knot.

Dustin Wedekind is the managing editor of **Beadwork** *magazine.*

Crazy Quilt Patchwork

Bethany Barry

8" L x 8½" W

I love the unpredictability of color, size, shape, and textures in crazy quilts, and the transformative possibilities offered by beads were just too good to pass up! Crazy quilting with seed beads is a great way to experiment with your favorite stitches: freeform, one-drop, two-drop, three-drop, etc., in right-angle weave or peyote, brick, and herringbone stitches. My finished bag measures 8" at the top and flares down in an A-line to 16" at the base. There are about eighty separate squares or shapes, done mostly with size 11° or 8° seed beads. This project was NOT finished overnight!

Materials

Assortment of seed beads in a variety of shapes, sizes, and colors

Size F Nymo beading thread

Notions

Size 12 beading or sharps needle

Scissors

Beeswax or Thread Heaven

Step 1: Using a yard of waxed thread and leaving a 4" tail, tie a tension bead at one end. Note: Work with a single strand for size 11° and a double strand for size 8° or 6° seed beads.

Step 2: String an even number of beads (20–40) in size 11°, 8°, or 6°, and make a flat peyote square patch.

Step 3: Make 10–20 patches in different sizes using various stitches. You can change bead sizes mid-square, as well as colors and shapes. You can have rectangles or strips, and you can use other shapes, such as ovals, circles, hearts, etc,. but the curved edges are more challenging to connect smoothly.

Consider the different textures you can create with the different beads and finishes—matte, metallic, silver-lined, opaque, clear, and color-lined—and choose accordingly as you make your squares.

Try adding small accent beads in place of the seed beads, such as 4mm round or rondelle miracle beads, small fiber-optic faceted, Austrian crystal faceted ovals, magatamas, cubes, triangles, hexes, and Balinese silver. Let your imagination go, and play with your own designs!

Step 4: Lay your patches out in a pattern for one side of the bag. Mine has forty patches per side. Try turning them different ways to see how they work best in terms of color, contrast, shape, and design. Don't worry if they don't fit together perfectly.

Step 5: Stitch the patches together, weaving the thread in and out of the beads to connect the sections. If there is a gap between two sections, fill the gap by sewing it closed with strands of seed beads. You can also use bigger beads combined with strands to fill the gaps—be creative and have fun, but make sure the strands are strong enough. Pass through all again to reinforce if necessary.

Step 6: As the pattern develops, add embellishments on the sections—strands of beads, small accent beads, picots, and various fringes.

Step 7: Make note of your patch sizes and numbers for the first side of the bag and make patches to create a second side.

Step 8: Stitch the sides together. Reinforce weak points with extra thread. When you've connected the sides and have reached the bottom, make an edge piece of free-form peyote to add interest and depth.

HANDLE

Step 9: Using flat even-count peyote stitch, make a strip 6" long by 2½" wide, or long enough to hold comfortably in your hand. I used 8°s in an assortment of colors for my bag. Stitch one end onto each side of the bag's center.

Step 10: Look over the finished bag to see if there are any places dying for a little extra color, charms, dangles, beaded flowers, or other festive ideas, and stitch them on. Weave in any extra thread and trim close to the work.

Bethany Barry teaches workshops internationally and lives in Vermont, where she beads happily in the woods. See her work at www. bethanybarry.com.

Landscape of Flowers

Jennifer Sevlie Diederich

8" L x 10" W (without handle)

This sunny bag will bring a smile to anyone who sees it. You can give it a different look by varying the purse fabric or by changing the embellishment beads, colors, and configurations.

Materials

40–50 size 6° or 8° beads or stones
Size 11° Japanese seed beads in 10–12 colors
1 yard fabric for the purse
⅛ yard complementary colored fabric for the sides of the purse
1 yard fabric for the purse lining
1 yard iron-on fusible interfacing
Size B Nymo beading thread in color to match the fabric
Brown paper lunch bag
Pair of wooden purse handles

Notions

Scissors
Ruler or tape measure
Iron
Fabric marker
Sewing pins
Size 11 straw John James Needles
Beeswax or Thread Heaven
Sewing machine (optional)

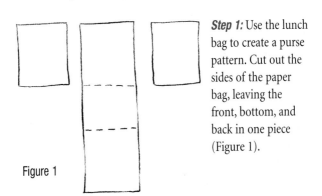

Step 1: Use the lunch bag to create a purse pattern. Cut out the sides of the paper bag, leaving the front, bottom, and back in one piece (Figure 1).

Figure 1

Step 2: Trace these paper bag shapes on the interfacing. Cut out the shapes.

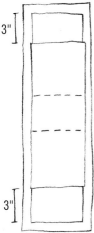

Figure 2

Step 3: Trace the pattern on the wrong side of the purse fabric. Add 3" to each end of the front, bottom, and back piece, and 1" all around for the seam allowance (Figure 2). Cut out the shape.

Step 4: Repeat Step 3 for the lining fabric.

Step 5: Trace and cut the side shapes using the side fabric, adding a 1" seam allowance; repeat for the lining fabric.

Step 6: Measure down 4" from the top of the large fabric piece. Iron the interfacing on the wrong side of the fabric at that measurement. The opposite side of the interfacing will be your beading area. Keeping in mind the 1" seam allowance on the sides, measure equal spaces apart on the right side of the fab-

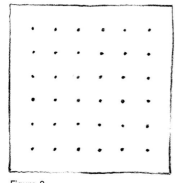

Figure 3

ric, marking with the fabric marker for the placement of each beaded flower center (Figure 3).

Step 7: Make a knot at the end of a length of thread. String a large bead and pass back through it three times to secure it. Pass up through the next mark. *String a large bead, pass back down through the fabric, make a knot, and pass up through the same bead. Repeat from * three times for each center bead. Repeat all for each mark on the fabric.

Step 8: Using a yard of thread, make a knot and *pass up through the fabric under and out from one of the large beads. *String 13 of a variety of size 11°s. Lay the strand out so it's not completely straight and pass through the fabric. The beads should hump up. Repeat from *, laying your strands at different angles.

String 10 size 11°s and place them between each of the longer strands.

String 6–8 size 11°s and place them between each strand so you have a complete flower (Figure 4).

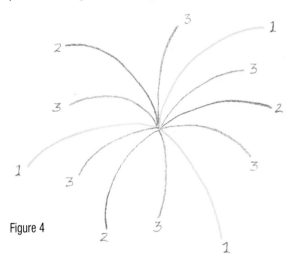

Figure 4

Knot on the wrong side of the fabric after completing each flower.

Repeat this step for each large bead sewn to the grid.

Step 9: Use a sewing machine or hand-sew one of the side pieces to the large piece. Put the right sides together and sew the bottom seam first and then the sides. Repeat for the other side piece.

Sew the lining together in the same way. Fit it inside the purse with wrong sides of the fabric together. Bring the purse fabric through the purse handle slot and hand-sew it to the inside of the purse. Hand-sew the top of the lining and the top of the purse together using small whipstitches.

Jennifer Sevlie Diederich has been working with fabric, beads, and fibers since she was knee-high to a grasshopper. It helps her forget the laundry. For information on wood handles, contact Jennifer at greetingsfromjupiter@attbi.com.

Metamorphosis Evening Clutch

Judi Wood

4" L X 5½" W

A favorite color and a scheflera tree inspired this clutch. On a road trip returning home the author saw a troop of invading caterpillars crossing the road and it was the perfect inspiration for the closure. Work in ranges of color to make your own colorway. Change the color scheme to give the bag a different seasonal effect.

Materials

50 gr of Delicas in several colors in one hue including one dark
Size 14°–15° seed beads
⅓ yard of satin in color to complement beads
Power Pro thread #10lb test
3" of dark twisted cord

Notions

Size 12 beading needle
Scissors
Oatmeal box
Fabric marker
Iron
Pinking shears
8" x 10" piece of cardboard
Soft cloth
Sewing machine (optional)

Step 1: Make the bag's body. Using a yard of thread and leaving a 4" tail, string 228 of the darkest Delicas. Tie a knot to create a circle and slip it over the oatmeal box. Work three rows of tubular peyote stitch using the darkest Delicas. Starting with the fourth row on the chart (Figure 1), work the

Figure 1

pattern and repeat it again on the other side of the tube. Note that the outlines of the leaf pattern are denoted but colors are not. Colors are your choice. When you've completed the pattern, leave the first few rounds in or remove them. Weave your thread through several beads to secure, and trim close to the work.

Step 2: Remove the beaded tube from the box. Fold the tube in half and start a new thread at one of the bottom corners. With the same dark color, make the bottom of the bag by working 7 rows of flat peyote across one side of the tube. Fit the edge to the beads on the other side of the tube. Lock the beads together and stitch them up like a zipper.

Step 3: Start a new thread at the top corner of the bag. Make a flap by working in flat odd-count peyote stitch across one half the bag using the chart.

Step 4: Lay your beadwork on top of the piece of cardboard and cut out the shape. Use the cardboard as a template to make a pattern on the satin. Use the fabric marker and trace the cardboard's shape onto the satin; leave a 1" seam allowance all around. Make another cutout of satin the same way. Cut out the shapes with pinking shears.

Cut two identical pocket-sized pieces of fabric. Press the fabric with a warm iron, folding under the 1" seam allowance.

With right sides together, sew the larger rectangles together at the seams. Leave a space so you can turn the lining inside out, and then stitch up the hole. Do the same with the smaller pocket-sized pieces of fabric.

Sew the pocket to the lining so that it will lie at the back of the purse.

Step 5: Fold the lining to resemble the purse's folds. Sew the sides together and place the lining inside the bag. Sew the lining to the bag. Begin by working at the edge across from the flap. Try to pass through every "up" bead. Continue along the sides of the purse and finally across the flap.

Step 6: Make the caterpillar by using the twisted cord. Wrap the cord with a dark color of Delicas, sewing through the cord to secure the beads. Decrease to three beads at each end. Weave into several beads to secure.

Using size 14°s, make short simple fringe to cover the entire body of the caterpillar except for the bottom. Make the bottom by leaving a strip about 4 beads wide down the center of the caterpillar. Sew the caterpillar close to the flap's edge.

Award winning artist Judi Wood is a frequent contributor to **Beadwork** *magazine. Find her work and show information at www.JudiWood.com.*

Opals and Abalone

Sandy Amazeen

3½" L x 2¾" W

This crocheted purse is a fun jumble of tiny opal chips and beads on metallic thread. If you've been building a supply of "bead soup," here's a great way to make use of it.

Materials

Tiny opal chips
Assorted size 6° and 8° beads to coordinate with the opal chips
Assorted accent beads
One skein of DMC size 5 silver metallic thread
Power Pro or Silamide thread

Notions

Size D crochet hook
Big Eye needle
Scissors
Sewing pins

BEADED DOUBLE CROCHET

To work beaded double crochet, yarn over, insert the hook, and work the first yarnover without slipping a bead down to the hook. The next two parts of the stitch are worked by sliding a bead down the yarn to the hook at the start of each yarnover. As the beads appear on the back side, it's a surprise when you work a couple of rows then turn the bag front side out for a peek.

Step 1: String 70" of assorted beads and chips on the metallic thread using the Big Eye needle.

Round 1: Chain 40 stitches without slipping beads into the stitches. Join the ends with a slipstitch, being careful to avoid any twists in the foundation ring.

Round 2: Chain 1 without slipping a bead; chain 2, slipping a bead in place on each. These three chains form the first double crochet and demonstrates how each new round is started. Work one beaded double crochet stitch in each chain of the foundation ring. When you have worked around the ring (40 double crochet stitches), join with a slipstitch.

Rounds 3–10: Repeat Round 2.

Round 11: Start decreasing to form the bottom of the bag. Begin the round, then work 6 double crochet stitches, skip 8 stitches, work 12 stitches, skip 8 stitches, work 6 stitches, and join the ring with a slipstitch.

Round 12: Begin the next round, then work 2 stitches, skip 8 stitches, work 4 stitches, skip 8 stitches, work 2 stitches, and join with a slipstitch. These series of missed stitches, 4 on the front and back sides, form the stepped-shape bottom. Cut the metallic thread leaving a 10" tail of bare thread. Use the tail and the Big Eye needle to sew the bottom closed (Figure 1). When all the openings are closed, make a knot, bury the thread, and trim close to the work.

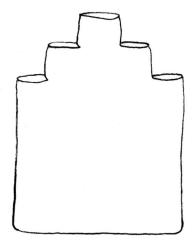

Figure 1

Step 2: Make hanging loops for the strap by tying on more metallic thread at the top right edge of the bag (Figure 2). You should still have some beads left on it. String an additional 2" if you don't. Mark the bag sides with a couple of pins, counting off 21 stitches for the back half and 19 for the front. Tie on the metallic thread and *chain 3 stitches, working the beads in the last two stitches. Double crochet two times. Repeat from * twice to form a hanging loop that is 3 double crochet stitches wide by 3 stitches long. Trim, leaving a 6" tail. Use the tail to sew the loop end to the other side of the bag. Repeat this step for the left side of the bag.

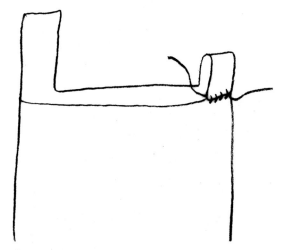

Figure 2

Step 3: Make the flap. Using a length of metallic thread without beads and leaving a 6" tail, tie on to the back of the bag, bead side facing up. Beginning immediately to the left of the hanging loop, chain 3 to equal the first double crochet. Work 14 double crochet stitches for a total of 15 stitches. At the end of the row, chain 3, turn and double crochet back. Do this once more for a total of three rows. At the end of row three, trim the thread leaving a 4" tail. Draw through the remaining open loop to tie off.

Count in 3 stitches and tie on another length of metallic thread. Work a row of 9 double crochet stitches. There should be 3 unworked stitches left on the end. Tie off. Count in 3 stitches again, tie on a new working thread, and work 3 double crochet. Again there should be 3 stitches left unworked at the end and the flap should now have a nice stepped shape.

To finish, work in any tails left hanging. Using a strong thread such as Power Pro or Silamide, create the strap and embellishments of your choice. Attach the strap through the loops.

Sandy Amazeen is a frustrated painter who taught herself weaving, spinning, knitting, stained glass, and jewelry making while traveling the continent. What refuses to come out of her head to appear on canvas is coaxed to life through a number of other outlets including beadwork, which she has enjoyed for thirty years.

Stitch Amulet Pouch

Jeannette Cook

2¾" L x 3½" W (without fringe)

This pouch is a great exploration of the various free-form sculptural peyote-stitch techniques. You can start out by planning the bag's basic size and colors, but just how the bag will turn out is a complete surprise!

Thanks to Vicki Star for the technique at the bottom of the bag.

Materials

> Assortment of seed beads in various sizes, shapes, and colors
> Size B Nymo or size A Silamide beading thread

Notions

> Size 12 beading or sharps needles
> Scissors

BOTTOM

Note: Work all rows and rounds in a variety of bead shapes, sizes, and colors. To achieve the look of the bag pictured here, begin by stringing the same kind of bead as the one you are exiting.

Rows 1 and 2: Using a yard of thread and leaving a 4" tail, string an even number of beads equaling the width you want the bottom of the pouch to be.
Row 3: Pass through the second-to-last bead strung and work peyote stitch across the row. You will end up with one bead with the tail thread exiting, another bead with your working thread exiting. Pass through the first bead strung in the first row (Figure 1).

Figure 1

SIDES

Round 1: You will now work in tubular peyote stitch. Work back to the other end. Pass through the last bead from Row 1 and back across the other side. Pass through the last bead of Row 3 and the first bead of this round (Figure 2).

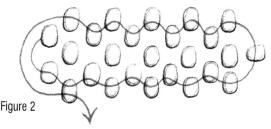

Figure 2

Round 2: Work across one side of the round. When you reach that side's end, pass through the end bead of the previous round. String a bead (the side bead) and pass through the end bead on the other side of the previous round. Continue to this side's end. String a bead and pass through the first bead of Row 1. String a bead and pass through the first bead of this round (Figure 3).

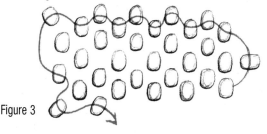

Figure 3

Round 3: Work across one side of the round. Pass through the side bead of the previous round. Work across the other side of the round. Pass through the closest side bead. String a bead. Pass through the next side bead (Figure 4).

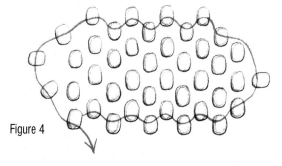

Figure 4

Rounds 4 and on: Work the rounds in tubular peyote stitch to make the bag as tall as you wish.

FRINGE

Make fringe along the bottom of the bag. Continue the color of the bead that the fringe originates from for a short length before adding accent beads. If one row of fringe looks too skimpy, add a second row just in front of the first row. Make all the fringes different lengths and put something special and different at the bottom of each fringe to keep the free-form theme consistent.

STRAP

Make a strap of your choice and stitch each end to the top corners of the bag.

STITCH NOTES

As you bead around the pouch and build up the sides, the pattern may begin to look too blocky or straight. To give the piece an undulating, flowing look, blend one color into the next. To blend, string the same bead as you are entering or exiting. Either way is fine. Be sure the old color flows without interruption into the new color. When you are changing from a large bead such as a cube or triangle to small bead such as a size 11° seed bead or a Delica, be sure to make up for size with quantity to prevent empty threads from showing.

You will notice that the areas where the larger beads are used get much taller than the smaller beads. Uneven edges are okay, but not radically uneven. To remedy the difference you can add beads on either side of the large bead, passing through the large bead without adding any more beads.

For added interest, try making little arches of beads over a low spot. As you come back around each time add a larger arch over the previous one. Keep your tension tight so the beads hold their shape. When you have enough beads, simply peyote stitch along the top arch.

You can add embellishments to hang over completed sections of beadwork.

Jeannette Cook has been working with beads as a wearable and fine art form for thirty-four years and teaching beading workshops for seventeen years. She is owner of Beady Eyed Women® and can be reached at www.jeannettecook.com.

Yellow Musette Bag

Marian Lyall

2½" L x 4" W

This cute little bead-knitted bag has a great three-dimensional effect. While the pattern shown here appears only on the middle flap, you can also knit it throughout. Knit the bag in three continuous sections separated by two fold rows.

Materials
1 ball of size 8 DMC 973 crochet cotton
1 hank of size 11° yellow AB seed beads
15mm yellow marble
Size B yellow beading thread

Notions
Pair of size 0000 knitting needles
Size 7 crochet hook
Size 12 beading needle
Tapestry needle

STITCH NOTES
The white spaces on the chart are knit stitches and don't contain beads. The chart shows only beaded rows, not unbeaded rows.

If beads are facing you, knit the row without adding beads. If beads are facing away from you, knit the row adding beads.

Abbreviations: k = knit, k1b = knit 1 bead, p = purl, yo = yarn over

INSIDE SECTION
String the yellow beads on the cotton by using a Bead Spinner or tying each bead strand to the cotton and transferring the beads.

Row 1: Make a slipknot and put your right needle in the loop. Move your first seed bead so it lies against the needle where the thread connects to the loop. Cast on normally. *Move

another bead up so it lies against the needle where the thread connects to the loop. Cast on normally. Repeat from * to make a total of 21 stitches. You should have 20 beads on the needle.

Row 2: With the beads facing away from you, k1. *Move a bead up against the needle where the thread connects to the stitch and k1b. Repeat from * across the row so you have 20 beads on the needle.

Row 3: With the beads facing you, cast on a stitch. Knit the row without adding beads. Cast on a stitch at the other end. Repeat Rows 2 and 3 until you have 40 beads on the needle, or 41 stitches. Finish with Row 15, a beaded row (Figure 1).

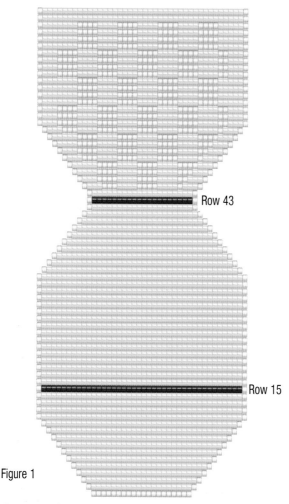

Row 43

Row 15

Figure 1

Row 16: With the beads facing you, *put the needle into the front of the stitch as if to purl the stitch. Move a bead up against the needle, yo, and p. Repeat from * across the row. This is a fold row.

Rows 17–36: Alternate rows of k1b across and k across. Knit the rows adding beads in every stitch.

Rows 37–41: Decrease each end of the nonbeaded rows until 21 stitches, or 20 beads, remain on the needle.

Row 42: Knit a beaded row.

Row 43: Repeat Row 16.

Row 44: Knit across.

Rows 45–53: *Cast on one beaded stitch. Follow the charted pattern, knitting across. Cast on one beaded stitch. Repeat from * across, making increases and following the chart.

Rows 54–68: Knit across, following the charted pattern. Cast off.

ASSEMBLY

Fold and pin the bag, bending the knitting at the fold rows, aligning the sides, and keeping the beads on the inside. Pin the body of the bag together: Count down two rows from the fold at Row 43 and pin the edge row of the front body of the bag. Smooth out this first fold, or Row 43 of the first section, so the beads show through. Sew the side seams together.

CHAIN

Crochet a beaded chain 30" long. Make a slip knot, *slide a bead up next to the hook, yo, and pull through. Repeat from *. Add beady beads (see page 114) to the ends. Use the crochet hook to attach the chain to each upper inside seam. Turn the bag inside out and pull the flap down.

FRONT FLAP

Using a yard of thread and the beading needle, weave into the bottom corner of the flap. With size 11°s create a strip of single drop flat peyote stitch that is the width of the flap edge and 9 rows long. Roll the strip and make a tube by stitching the sides together like a zipper. Weave through several beads to secure and trim the thread close to the work.

BEADED MARBLE

Round 1: Using a yard of beading thread and leaving a 4" tail, string 8 size 11°s. Tie in a knot to form a foundation circle.

Round 2: *String 3 size 11°s, skip 1 bead on the foundation circle, and pass into the third bead. Repeat from * until you have 4 nets. Exit from the first 2 beads added in this round.

Round 3: *String 5 size 11°s. Skip one bead on the net from Round 2 and pass through the center bead of the net. Repeat from * all around.

Round 4: *String 7 size 11°s. Skip two beads on the next net of Round 3 and pass through the center bead. Repeat from * all around.

Rounds 5–7: Repeat Round 4 until half your marble is covered.

Round 8: Repeat Round 3.

Round 9: Repeat Round 2.

Round 10: Weave through each middle bead of the net in the previous row and draw tight. String 6 beads and secure through the bead across the small circle to serve as a hook. To further embellish your bead, thread 3 or 4 beads and string them across various points in the netting to make a more intricate design.

BEADY BEADS

Make two.

Using a yard of thread and leaving a 4" tail, string 6 size 11°s. Work flat peyote stitch for 7 rows. Fold so the beads lock and stitch together like a zipper.

Marian Lyall has been knitting from the age of four and beading since she was twelve. She is completely addicted to bead knitting and welcomes your thoughts and comments at melizy@telus.net.

Crystal Mesh Reticule

Chris Prussing

4½" L x 4¾" W

Transform an ordinary velveteen drawstring pouch into a sparkling beaded reticule to hang from a sash, belt, or wrist. Best of all, the beadwork is attached to the pouch at just a few spots, so it can be detached and recycled at whim.

Materials

- 1,200 3mm transparent gray fire-polished faceted round beads (A)
- 400 3mm gold-lined fire-polished faceted round beads (B)
- 4mm cream glass pearls
- Size 11° gold seed beads
- PowerPro 10# test
- Lined gray velveteen drawstring pouch
- Hypo-tube cement

Notions

- Size 10 beading needles
- Scissors

Begin by using 2 yards of thread with a needle on each end. String 4 B on the right needle and move them to the center of the thread. Pass the left needle back through the fourth bead strung and pull tight to make a diamond.

Step 1: *String 3 A on the right thread. String 3 A and 1 B on the left. Pass the right needle back

115

through the B strung on the left. String 1 B on the right needle, and 2 B on the left. Pass the right needle back through the last bead strung on the left. Repeat from * four times.

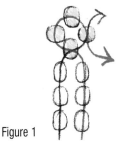

Figure 1

String 3 A on the right thread, and 3 A and 1 B on the left. Pass the right needle back through the B strung on the left. String 3 B on the left needle, and pass the right needle back through the last bead strung on the left thread (Figure 1).

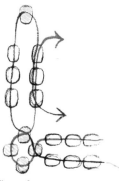

Figure 2

Move your work a quarter turn. Use the left needle to string 3 A, 1 B, and 3 A. Pass the right needle back through the last 3 A strung (Figure 2).

Step 2: Move your work a quarter turn. *Pass the right needle through 3 A on the adjacent row as shown. String 6 A on the left thread and pass the right needle back through the last 3 A strung on the left (Figure 3). Pass the right needle through the 1 B on the adjacent row. String 1 B and 3 A on the left thread. Pass the right needle back through the 3 A strung on the left. Repeat from * four times.

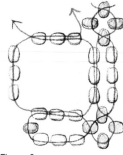

Figure 3

Pass the right needle through the 3 A on the adjacent row. String 6 A on the left thread, and pass the right needle back through the last 3 A strung on the left. Pass the right needle through the 1 B on the adjacent row, and string 3 A and 1 B on the right needle. Pass the left needle back through the 1 B strung on the right (Figure 4).

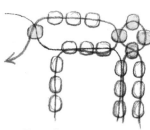

Figure 4

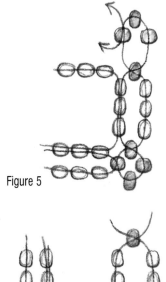

Move your work a quarter turn. String 3 B on the right thread and pass the left needle back through the last B strung on the right (Figure 5).

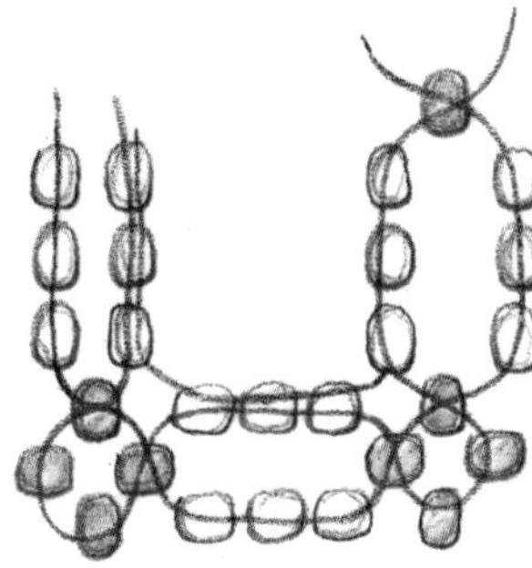

Step 3: Move your work a quarter turn. *Pass the left needle through the 3 A on the adjacent row. String 3 A and 1 B on the right thread and pass the left needle back through the 1 B just strung (Figure 6). Pass the left needle through the 1 B on the adjacent row. String 2 B on the right thread and pass the left needle back through the last B strung. Repeat from * four times.

Figure 5

Figure 6

Pass the left needle through the 3 A on the adjacent row. String 3 A and 1 B on the right thread and pass the left needle back through the 1 B strung. Pass the left needle through the 1 B on the adjacent row and string 2 B on the left thread. Pass the right needle back through the last B strung on the left.

Move your work a quarter turn. Use the left needle to string 3 A, 1 B, and 3 A. Pass the right needle back through the last 3 A strung.

Step 4: Repeat Steps 2 and 3 six times to create a grid of 36 units of double matrix right-angle-weave beadwork.

Make two grids.

Step 5: Arrange each matrix as a diamond shape and lay each against the pouch. Sew the top corner of the matrix to the pouch back and forth through the unit and pouch several times. Sew the matrices to one another at the corners, and attach to the bag if necessary to achieve an attractive drape. In the purse illustrated, an additional tab of 6-and-4 weave was added to make the grid better fit the pouch. (Figure 7).

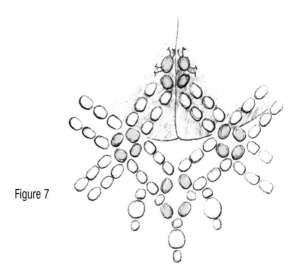

Figure 7

Step 6: Add your choice of fringe along the lower edges of the matrices. The sample uses one gold seed bead, one pearl, and one gold seed bead, with each fringe coming from between two of the matrix beads.

Step 7: Decorate the drawstring ends by covering the knots with your favorite style of beaded bead. Or untie the drawstring knots, add a large bead to each cord, and retie the knots. The beaded bead in the sample is beaded over both the cord knots.

Chris Prussing is a bead artist who can be contacted at www.rightangleweave.com.

One Needle R.A.W. Bag

julia s. pretl

7 L x 5 ¾ W

The tenacious beadworker will rejoice after making this gorgeous bag with right-angle weave.

Materials

- 350 gr size 11° Czech brown iris metallic seed beads
- 17 size 1 bugle beads
- 80 size 3 bugle beads
- 17 tiger eye chips
- 2 square feet of tan linen
- 1 roll of fusible adhesive
- Size B beading thread to match beads

Notions

- Size 12 beading or sharps needle
- Scissors
- Fabric pencil

BODY

Step 1: Make a fabric of one-needle right-angle weave with each unit using 2 beads per side. The finished fabric will be a rectangle 37 units across by 106 units down.

SIDE

Step 2: Secure a new thread to exit the top of the thirty-ninth 2-bead set. String 4 beads and pass up through the edge of the fortieth set. Pull tight to form a corner that will join the front and bottom of the bag. Pass through the fortieth and thirty-ninth units, the last four beads, and into the forty-first unit.

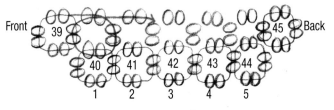

Front 39 40 41 42 43 44 45 Back
1 2 3 4 5

Bottom

Work three more units along the bottom of the bag. Join the fifth new unit to the forty-fifth unit with just two beads to form the back corner of the bag (Figure 1).

Step 3: Continue to work 5-unit rows of right-angle weave up the side of the bag. Reinforce the last row (at the top of the front of the bag) by passing through the edge beads a few times. Continue the 5-unit rows to form the strap [Step 4]. Step 2: Beginning at a top corner of the body, count down sixty-one 2-bead sets. Securely weave in a new thread and enter then exit the sixty-second 2-bead set from the top of the set.

STRAP

Step 4: Make 5-unit rows off one side of the bag until you have a narrow strap approximately 18" long or half the length of the strap. Weave your thread into your beadwork. Repeat on the other side of your bag but do not weave your thread into your work.

Check to see that both sides are the same by measuring the length of one side and strap, beginning at the bottom side corner of the bag, and then the other.

Making sure that the two strap pieces aren't twisted, complete one more row to join the two strap ends. You will be adding only 2 beads per side because the top and bottom sides of each unit already exist in the strap ends. Weave your thread into your beadwork to finish.

LINING

Step 5: Using a ruler, measure and draw a rectangle the size of the body of your bag on your linen. Now measure and draw another rectangle ½" wider all the way around your first rectangle. Cut along the outer rectangle.

Step 6: At a short end of the rectangle, fold at the drawn line so the line is inside the fold and hidden. Iron at this line. Cut a strip of fusible adhesive and sandwich it inside the fold. Iron to seal the hem.

Repeat this step on the other short end and then on each of the long ends.

Step 7: Repeat Steps 11 and 12 so you have two identical hemmed rectangles.

Step 8: Whipstitch the rectangles together with the hemmed sides facing one another.

Step 9: Repeat Steps 11 and 12 using the measurement of your sides and strap. Depending on the width of your fabric, you may have to make each strap lining in two segments and sew them together. Due to the narrow width, the strap lining will be rather thick. The thickness is good because it strengthens the strap.

Step 10: Measure the distance of one of the short ends of the bag lining and then measure and mark the same distance from the same corner along the long edge. Butt a strap lining edge perpendicularly against the point of the bag lining so that the corner touches the mark. Mark the spot where the other corner of the strap lining hits the bag lining. Mark and measure the other long edge of the bag.

Pin and whipstitch the strap lining to the bag lining so that the corner points correspond. Stop sewing when you get to the flap portion of the lining.

Slide the lining into the bag.

Step 11: Sew the lining into the bag along the front top of the bag, both sides of the strap, and the 2 sides of the flap (not the end) by sewing through each 2-bead set and then through the fabric between each 2-bead set. There is no "wrong" way to do this. Just be sure that the beads lie flat against the lining.

INNER FRINGE
Step 12: Thread a needle and tie a small knot at the end of the thread. Sew between the layers of the flap lining at the corner. Exit the needle at the corner of the flap. Pull so that the knot slips between the 2 layers. The thicker fabric at the corner of the bag should stop the knot. Be careful not to catch the beaded portion of the flap.

*String 35 size 11°s, 1 size 3 bugle, then 1 size 11°. Skip the last size 11° and pass back up through the rest of the beads. Sew through the edge of the flap lining once again but about ⅛" from the first fringe. Repeat from * until you reach the other corner of the flap lining.

OUTER FRINGE

Step 13: Weave a new thread into the flap portion of the bag so that it enters the outer corner 2-bead set and exits the set pointing in (toward the rest of the bag edge).

*String 5 size 11°s, 1 size 1 bugle, 10 size 11°s, 1 tiger eye chip, and 5 size 11°s. Pass back up through the first 5 size 11°s of the 10 strung and the bugle, then string 5 more size 11°s. Pass through the third 2-bead set on the edge of the flap, skipping the second one. Repeat for the other corner of the flap and weave thread into beadwork.

---

julia s. pretl has lived in Baltimore her entire life. She majored in graphic design at the Baltimore Institute College of Art before discovering beads in 1990.

Tips

STARTING A NEW THREAD

There's no doubt that you'll run out of thread as you work on your necklaces that use off-loom stitches. It's easy to begin a new thread. There are a couple of solutions. I prefer the first way because it's stronger.

Solution 1: Tie off your old thread when it's about 4" long by making a simple knot between beads. Pass through a few beads and pull tight to hide the knot. Weave through a few more beads and trim the thread close to the work. Start the new thread by tying a knot between beads and weaving through a few beads. Pull tight to hide the knot. Weave through several beads until you reach the place to begin again.

Solution 2: Here's how to end your old thread without tying a knot. Weave the thread in and out, around and around, through several beads and then trim it close to the work. Begin a new thread the same way, weaving the end of the thread in and out, around and around, and through several beads until you reach the place to begin again.

PASS THROUGH VS. PASS BACK THROUGH

Pass through means to move your needle in the same direction as the beads have been strung. Pass back through means to move your needle in the opposite direction.

TENSION BEAD

A tension bead holds your work in place. To make one, string a bead larger than those you are working with, then pass through the bead again, making sure not to split your thread. The bead will be able to slide along, but will still provide tension to work against.

Techniques

Peyote stitch

This stitch can also be referred to as gourd stitch.

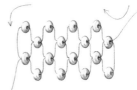
Peyote stitch

One-drop peyote begins by stringing an even number of beads to create the first two rows. Begin the third row by stringing one bead and passing through the second-to-last bead of the previous rows. String another bead and pass through the fourth-to-last bead of the previous rows. Continue adding one bead at a time, passing over every other bead of the previous rows.

Two-drop peyote is worked the same as above, but with two beads at a time instead of one.

Peyote stitch increase

Make a *mid-project increase* by working a two-drop over a one-drop in one row. In the next row work a one-drop peyote between the two-drop. For a smooth increase, use very narrow beads for both the two-drop and the one-drop between.

Peyote stitch increase

Peyote stitch decreases

To make a *row-end decrease*, simply stop your row short and begin a new row. To make a hidden row-end decrease, pass through the last bead on a row. Weave your thread between two beads of the previous row, looping it around the thread that connects the beads. Pass back through the last bead of the row just worked and continue across in regular flat peyote. To make a *mid-project decrease*, simply pass thread through two beads without adding a bead in the "gap." In the next row, work a regular one-drop peyote over the decrease. Keep tension taut to avoid holes.

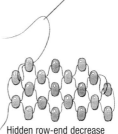
Hidden row-end decrease

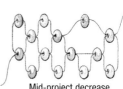
Mid-project decrease

Peyote stitch odd count

Begin by stringing an odd number of beads (our example shows five). These beads will become the first and second rows. Begin the next row by adding a bead and passing through the second-to-last bead just strung, bead 4 in our example. Continue as with even-count peyote. When you reach the end of the row, pass through beads 1, 2, and 3. Pass through the second-to-last bead in what has now become the third row. Pass back through beads 2 and 1 (in that order). Pass through the last bead added in row 3. Continue across row 4 in regular peyote. Start row 5 as you began row 3. At the end of row 5, exit from the last bead added and loop thread through the outer edge threads (not beads) of the previous row. Pass back through the last bead added and continue across the row adding one bead at a time.

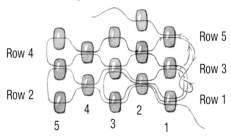

Peyote stitch odd count

Square stitch

Begin by stringing a row of beads. For the second row, string 2 beads, pass through the second-to-last bead of the first row, and back through the second bead of those just strung.

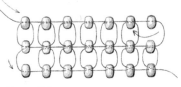

Square stitch

Continue by stringing 1 bead, passing through the third-to-last bead of the first row, and back through the bead just strung. Repeat this looping technique across to the end of the row. *To make a decrease,* weave thread through the previous row and exit from the bead adjacent to the place you want to decrease. Continue working in square stitch.

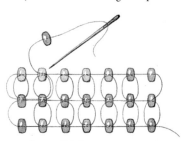

Square stitch decrease

Single-needle right-angle weave

The illustration refers to bead positions, not bead numbers.

Row 1: String four base beads. Pass through beads in positions 1, 2, and 3. The bead in position 3 will become the bead in position 1 in the next group. String 3 beads. Pass through bead in position 3 of last group (now position 1 of this group), bead in position 2 and bead in position 3 (now position 1 of next group). String 3 beads. Continue working in this pattern until the row is to a desired length. In the last group, pass through beads in positions 1, 2, 3, and 4.

Row 2: String 3 beads. Pass through bead in position 4 of previous group and bead in position 1 of this group. String 2 beads. Pass through bead in position 2 of Row 1, bead in position 1 of previous group, and the beads just added. Pass through bead in position 4 of Row 1. String 2 beads. Pass through bead in position 2 of previous group and bead in position 4 of Row 1. Pass through first bead just added. String 2 beads. Pass through bead in position 2 of Row 1, bead in position 1 of previous group, and the first bead just added.

Row 3: Repeat Row 2.

Loomwork

After warping your loom, use a separate thread ("weft") to string the number of beads needed for the first row. Bring the weft thread under the warp threads and push the beads up with your finger so there is one bead between each of two warp threads. Hold the

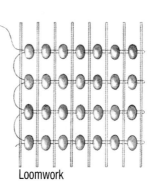

Loomwork

beads in place, bring the weft thread over the warp threads, and pull back through all the beads. Repeat these steps for each row.

Brick stitch

Begin by creating a foundation row in ladder stitch (see below). String one bead and pass through the closest exposed loop of the foundation row. Pass back through the same bead and continue, adding one bead at a time.

Brick stitch

Back stitch

Back stitch (also known as "return stitch" and "running stitch"). Begin by passing the needle through the fabric, from wrong side to right side, at the place where the first bead is to go. String a bead and pass the needle back through the fabric to the left of the bead. Bring the needle back through the fabric to the right of the bead, pass back through the bead, and back down through the fabric. Continue with one backstitch per bead. You can sew up to three beads per stitch by stringing three beads and backstitching only through the third as shown.

Back stitch

Couching

Also known as "two-thread spot stitch," this technique uses two threaded needles. Begin by passing the needle through the fabric, from wrong side to right side, at the place where the first bead is to go. Thread a number of beads and lay them onto the cloth in your chosen design. With the second threaded needle, come up through the cloth, over the thread between two beads, and back down through the cloth. Repeat this procedure until all the beads lie flat.

Couching

Lane stitch (aka Lazy stitch)

Pass the needle through the fabric from wrong to right side at the place where the first bead is to go. String the number of beads desired for a row, take a stitch so you exit at the place where the next row will be.

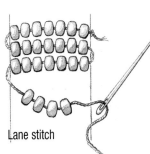

Lane stitch

Blind stitch

This stitch does not show on the right side of the fabric. Place them ¼ to ½ inch (6 mm to 1.3 cm) apart. Press the hem to the wrong side, making a double fold. Secure the sewing thread inside folded hem. As you bring the thread through the hem, insert the needle through the loop of thread floating between the first and second stitches. Take the next stitch with the thread between the two stitches straight but not tight. Work across the hem.

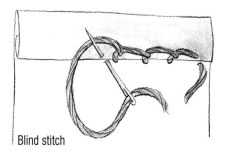

Blind stitch

Whipstitch

Take a stitch through the fabric from wrong side to right side. Move your needle over ⅛" and take another stitch from wrong side to right side. Continue across.

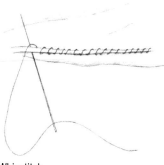

Whipstitch

Knitting Techniques

Bead knitting

Bead knitting

Bead knitting, knitting one bead into one stitch, is the technique to use for knitting charted designs. Insert the needle into the stitch to be knit as usual, slide the bead up against the needle, and pull the bead through to the front as you complete the stitch.

Beaded Knitting

Beaded knitting is a technique that leaves beads lying on the thread between two knit stitches. This means beads show on

the back of the work. When beads lie between two purl stitches, they show on the front of the work.

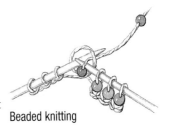

Beaded knitting

Work the stitch, slide the bead(s) up right against the stitch just worked, and work the next stitch.

Slip Stitch

Slip stitches are an easy method for decreasing or for use in selvedges or decorative stitches. To slip a stitch is simply to move it from one needle to another.

To slip a stitch knitwise, insert the right needle into the first stitch on the left needle as if you were going to knit it, then slip the stitch off the left needle onto the right needle.

To slip a stitch purlwise, insert the right needle into the first stitch on the left needle as if you were going to purl it, then slip the stitch off the left needle onto the right needle.

Yarnover Increase

The simplest of increase methods, the yarnover increase is usually specified for openwork patterns. This decorative increase produces a visible hole that is the basis for knitted lace. Many knitters mistakenly wrap

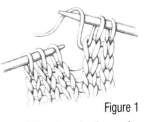

Figure 1

the yarn in the wrong direction, especially when they're working a yarnover between a knit and purl stitch. Although the visual difference is slight, incorrect yarnovers can produce different-sized holes. To make all yarnovers consistent, it is important that you work the motion separately from the next stitch and that your motion always brings the yarn from below the needle in front, around and over the top of the needle, ending below the needle in the back, at which point the yarn is positioned for the next stitch. On the following row, work the yarnover as a normal stitch (unless otherwise directed). Work a yarnover between two knit stitches by wrapping the yarn around the needle from front to back (Figure 1). Work a yarnover after a knit stitch and before a purl stitch by bringing the yarn to the front under the needle, around the top of the needle to the back, and then under the needle to the front.

Between two purl stitches, work the yarnover by bringing the yarn over the top of the needle (front to back), then around the bottom of the needle and to the front again. Work a yarnover after a purl stitch and before a knit stitch by bringing the yarn over the top of the needle (again, from front to back), then around to the back of the needle.

Crochet Techniques

Bead crochet

Bead crochet in rounds yields a very dense, continuous surface. To work a bead in single crochet, insert the hook into the back of the stitch, put the yarn over the hook and draw a loop through—you now have two loops on the hook. Slide a bead up to the loops, wrap yarn over

Bead crochet

the hook, and draw the yarn through the loops. The bead will be fixed to the back side of the crocheted work.

Chain (ch)—Make a slipknot on hook. Yarn over, draw through loop of slip knot. Repeat process drawing the thread through last loop formed.

Bead chain (bch)—Push bead up against work. Yarn over beyond the bead and pull loop through.

Beaded single crochet (bsc)—Insert hook into indicated stitch, yarn over, draw loop through stitch, pull bead up close to stitch, yarn over, draw thread through two loops on hook.

Beaded double crochet (bdc)—Yarn over, insert hook into indicated stitch, yarn over, draw loop through stitch, pull bead up close to stitch, yarn over, draw thread through two loops, pull bead up close to stitch, yarn over, draw thread through remaining two loops on hook.

Bead triple crochet (btr)—Yarn over twice, insert hook into indicated stitch, yarn over, draw loop through stitch, (pull

bead up close to stitch, yarn over, draw thread through 2 loops on hook) 3 times.

Double crochet (dc)—Yarn over, insert hook into indicated stitch, yarn over, draw loop through stitch, yarn over, draw thread through two loops, yarn over, draw thread through remaining two loops on hook.

Increase (inc)—Add one stitch of the type specified.

Decrease (dec)—In a row, decrease one stitch of the type specified.

Single crochet (sc)—Insert hook into indicated stitch, yarn over, draw loop through stitch, yarn over, draw thread through two loops on hook.

Slip stitch (ss)—Insert hook into indicated stitch, yarn over, drawn thread through stitch and loop on hook.

Triple crochet (tr)—Yarn over twice, insert hook into indicated stitch, (yarn over, draw loop through stitch, draw thread through two loops), three times.

Bead crochet rope

Bead crochet rope makes a great finish or a strap for other bead-work. Make an initial chain of four (or more) stitches, leaving a bead in each chain stitch by

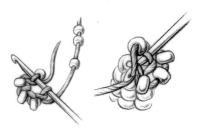

Bead crochet rope

sliding a bead close to the hook before making each stitch. Form a ring of beaded stitches by inserting the hook into the first chain stitch, under the thread carrying the bead. Move the bead to the right of the hook.

Slide a new bead down close to the hook and work a slip stitch by pulling a loop of thread through both the loops on the hook. Make a slip stitch with a bead into each of the remaining chain stitches to complete the first round. Continue working beaded slip stitches in a spiral to the length desired.

Fringe Techniques

Simple fringe

Exit from your base. String as many beads as you wish the finished length of the fringe leg to be. Skipping the last bead strung, pass back through all of the beads. Pass through the base and exit from the next spot on the base. Repeat across to make many legs of fringe.

Looped fringe

Exit from your base. String enough seed beads to form a loop. Pass through the base near the top of the loop and exit ¼" along the base. String the same amount of beads as in the first loop. Pass through the first loop from back to front (or front to back; just be consistent). Repeat across to make a row of loops.

Kinky fringe

Anchor the thread in your fabric or beadwork base. String 15 to 20 beads. This is your base row. Skip the last bead and pass back through 6 to 8 beads. Pull the thread taut. String 6 to 8 beads. Skip the last bead and pass back through the beads just strung. Pass back through 6 to 8 beads of the base row, moving toward the top. Repeat Steps 2 and 3 until you reach the end of the base row.